The
MANIPULATORS

Also by Everett L. Shostrom and Dan Montgomery

God in Your Personality (1986)

Healing Love (1978)

By Everett L. Shostrom

Actualizing Therapy,
with Lila and Robert Knapp (1976)

Between Man and Woman,
with James Kavanaugh (1972)

Freedom to Be (1973)

From Manipulator to Master (1983)

Man, the Manipulator (1967, 1968)

The Manipulator and the Church,
with Maxie D. Dunnam and Gary J. Herbertson (1969)

Therapeutic Psychology,
with Lawrence Bramme and Phillip Abrego (1989)

By Dan Montgomery

Courage to Love (1980)

The MANIPULATORS

EVERETT L.
SHOSTROM &
DAN
MONTGOMERY

ABINGDON PRESS

Nashville

The Manipulators

Copyright © 1990, 1967 by Abingdon Press

This book is printed on acid-free paper.

Library of Congress Cataloging-in-Publication Data

SHOSTROM, EVERETT L., 1921-
    The manipulators / Everett L. Shostrom. Dan Montgomery.
        p.   cm.
    ISBN 0-687-23075-6 (alk. paper)
    1. Manipulative behavior. 2. Self-actualization (Psychology)
I. Montgomery, Dan, 1946-   . II. Title.
BF632.5.S46   1990
158'.2—dc20   90-33395
                                                              CIP

MANUFACTURED IN THE UNITED STATES OF AMERICA

Three psychologists were the inspiration for this book:

Frederick Perls, who encouraged us to develop a classification system of manipulation. His topdog, underdog theory provided the schema for the manipulative types;

Carl Rogers, whose psychology of unconditional positive regard helped us to develop a deep respect for our clients and provided us with the best method for promoting the health in our clients;

Abraham Maslow, whose study of the characteristics of self-actualized individuals gave us not only the blue-print of health, but also an abiding belief in the essential goodness of each person. This belief underlies our system of psychotherapy.

The Manipulators builds on the ideas of these three men. We wish to express our gratitude and affection for them, and to each of them we dedicate this book.

Everett L. Shostrom, Ph.D.
Dan Montgomery, Ph.D.

Acknowledgments

We wish to express our gratitude to our families and friends and to our many associates and clients, whose lives touched our lives and whose ideas helped us to grow. We also wish to thank Sharon Kay Shostrom for putting the technical ideas of this book into conversational style. We also wish to acknowledge the contributions of John Wesley Noble to the book *Man, the Manipulator*, of which this book is a revision. And finally, we are especially grateful to Abingdon Press, for patience and expert guidance in the completion of *The Manipulators*.

Contents

List of Figures

I. The Basic Principles

CHAPTER 1

Introduction

Man, the Manipulator, first published in 1967, described ways in which people manipulate each other: treat each other as "things," exploit, use and control each other in ways that defeat the whole purpose of their being together. Eight manipulative types were described: the four "topdog" manipulators—the *Judge*, the *Bully*, the *Calculator*, and the *Dictator*—and the four "underdog" manipulators—the *Weakling*, the *Clinging Vine*, the *Nice Guy*, and the *Protector* (see Fig. 1). These manipulators were described as follows:

1. The *Dictator* exaggerates self-strength. This person dominates, orders, quotes authorities, and does anything that will control victims. Variations of the Dictator are Mother Superiors, Father Superiors, Rank Pullers, the Boss, and Junior Gods.

2. The *Weakling* is usually the Dictator's victim, the polar opposite. The Weakling develops great skills in coping with the Dictator. The Weakling exaggerates his or her sensitivity, usually forgets, doesn't hear, and is passively silent. Variations of the Weakling are the Worrier, the "Stupid-Like-a-Fox," the Giver-Upper, the Confused, and the Withdrawer.

3. The *Calculator* exaggerates control. This person deceives, lies, and constantly tries to outwit and control other people. Variations of the Calculator are the High-pressure Salesperson, the Seducer, the Poker Player, the Con Artist, the Blackmailer, and the Intellectualizer.

4. The *Clinging Vine* is the polar opposite of the Calculator. The Clinging Vine exaggerates his or her dependency. This is the person who wants to be led, fooled, and taken care of, letting others do the work. Variations of the Clinging Vine are the Parasite, the Crier, the Perpetual Child, the Hypochondriac, the Attention Demander, and the Helpless One.

5. The *Bully* exaggerates aggression, cruelty, and unkindness. This person controls by implied threats of some kind. The Bully is the Humiliator, the Hater, the Tough Guy, the Threatener.

6. The *Nice Guy* exaggerates caring and love and kills with kindness. In one sense, the Nice Guy is much harder to cope with than the Bully—you can't fight a Nice Guy! Curiously, in any conflict with the Bully, the

Nice Guy almost always wins! Variations of the Nice Guy are the Pleaser, the Nonviolent One, the Nonoffender, the Noninvolved One, the Virtuous One, the Never-Ask-for-What-You-Want One, and the Organization Man.

7. The *Judge* exaggerates criticalness. This person distrusts everybody and is blameful, resentful, and slow to forgive. Variations of the Judge are the Know-It-All, the Blamer, the Deacon, the Resentment Collector, the Should-er, the Shamer, the Comparer, the Vindicator, and the Convictor.

8. The *Protector* is the opposite of the Judge. The Protector exaggerates support and is nonjudgmental to a fault. This person spoils others, is over-sympathetic, and refuses to allow those he or she protects to stand up and grow for themselves. Instead of caring for his or her own needs, the Protector cares only for others' needs. Variations of the Protector are the Mother Hen, the Defender, the Embarrassed-for-Others, the Fearful-for-Others, the Sufferer-for-Others, the Martyr, the Helper, and the Unselfish One.

Such names served not only to describe the types of manipulative styles but to underscore the fact that manipulation is a caricature of authentic human expression in much the same way that a cartoon character is—but in a human life, especially your own, a caricature is no laughing matter.

The million or more people who read *Man, the Manipulator* found manipulators everywhere: in their families, among their friends and co-workers, and perhaps even within themselves. The truth is that we

Figure 1
The Manipulative Caricatures

are all manipulators some of the time. We all use deceptive means to get the particular response we want from another person. Uncertain that we are acceptable as we truly are, we show the "face" we think others want to see; we don the mask of the manipulator. For some of us, the mask is sinister. It's the mask of the "topdog," and we use it to play tough, judgmental, overbearing, or mean. For the rest of us, the mask is angelic. It's the mask of the "underdog," and we use it to play helpless, protective, gullible, or adoring.

As manipulators, we refuse to allow ourselves to be who we are. At the same time, we refuse to allow others to be who they are. Instead we get stuck and stay stuck in unsatisfying relationships.

You'll be taking a kind of journey with the help of this book, and it will be a dual one. It's as if you're traveling on a highway that has two lanes going in your direction, and you have the ability to switch from one lane to the other as the situation calls for.

The dual lanes represent the two kinds of relationships you have in your life. The first is your relationship with yourself. Kierkegaard says it means "to be that self which you truly are" (*The Sickness Unto Death*). It consists of how you feel about yourself, what you think about yourself, and how you treat yourself. The second is the relationship you have with the people around you. It has to do with the way you talk to and treat people. It involves the degree to which you can *listen* to others and understand them. It is a simple process, but it has profound implications.

Learning about yourself is interesting, but it is useless unless you can apply what you learn to your relationships with others. Likewise, improving your relations with others is almost impossible to do without first improving your sense of self.

On this journey, both lanes are wide open, and you can travel in one, the other, or both lanes at the same time. On this highway, traffic laws don't apply, but road signs do. The kind of signs you will encounter on this journey are about yourself—the principles of human experience and expression that can guide you away from self-defeating "dead-ends" toward freer self-expression and improved personal relationships.

One principle essential to this book is that of "polarities." A polarity exists at the two ends of a continuum. A polarity is the manifestation of two opposing tendencies, such as "yes" at one end and "no" at the other. This principle of polarities is useful to understanding your internal "road map" of thoughts, feelings, actions, and bodily sensations.

Thoughts, feelings, actions, and bodily sensations can be summarized as four basic conditions of human experience on two polarities. Love opposing anger, and strength opposing weakness. Or anger opposing love, and weakness opposing strength.

Like everyone else, you are capable of both love and anger, and you are strong as well as weak. Love isn't better than anger, and strength isn't better than weakness. They are simply conditions of your existence, opposing forces in your make-up. But the polarities of love and anger, weakness and strength, have a great deal to do with your manipulations, and they will play a major role in your overcoming them.

Another principle in this book is the therapeutic system called "Actualizing Therapy," whose roots can be found in the work of Abraham Maslow. The term *actualizing* can be used interchangeably with such words as *authentic, real,* and *genuine,* as opposed to such words as *phony, manipulative,* and *deceitful.* The goal of Actualizing Therapy is to increase authenticity and to decrease manipulation in interpersonal relationships.

HURT, FEAR, AND UNSATISFYING RELATIONSHIPS

With our first cries, steps, and words as babies we were set on the road to manipulation, refining and personalizing our styles as we grew into adulthood. We learned a lot from experts along the way—our parents, brothers and sisters, playmates, and teachers. But the most effective teacher of manipulation was our fear.

It's fun to observe the machinations of the person at the office who attempts to "brown-nose" the way to the top of the corporate ladder, only to be passed over for the BIG PROMOTION by the young MBA graduate hired just six months earlier, whom the "brown-nose" had been training. Unless, of course, you happen to be that person!

If you are that person, you have spent your career—your whole life—being helpful, ingratiating, pleasing, placating, noncombative, agreeable, and passive. You managed to avoid conflict at all costs—all because you were afraid. You were afraid people wouldn't like you. You were afraid someone might be angry with you if you said no. You had been so nice, how could such a bad thing happen to you!

What about that young MBA graduate you were training who got your promotion? It was quite satisfying when she didn't last a year in the job you wanted (Of course, you would never say such a thing at the office). You could see through her phoniness. You knew she only got the promotion because she had made

17

the boss think that you were incompetent and that the rest of the staff was lazy and needed a "firm hand." The entire office had been reeling from her angry outbursts whenever anything went wrong. Even when nothing was wrong, she was nasty and accusing. Everyone avoided her like the plague. No wonder she finally got fired.

She had spent her short career and whole life being angry, blaming everyone but herself for failings, real and imaginary. Like you, she was afraid. But unlike you, she was afraid that if she wasn't careful she might get too close to others, become dependent on them, and get rejected and hurt. She wanted to get them before they got her. But they got her anyway. She was alone and angry and afraid.

A neighbor of hers, hearing she was unemployed and looking for a job, stopped by to offer his assistance. Actually, he had been trying to get a chance to ask her out, but had never been able to engage her in a conversation of any length. She was always brusque and in a hurry. Now he had his opportunity. As he knocked on her door, he sensed she was feeling defeated and weak.

"I heard you were fired from your job last week and thought you might need cheering up. How about dinner tonight? There's this great French restaurant downtown. You've probably never been there—it's expensive. Great place. I entertain my clients there quite often. It's about time you found out how the other half lives. How about it? I'll pick you up in my new Porsche. You probably know that I'm head of sales now for the whole western division. I'm pretty busy, keeping track of everything. Can't trust those doltish salesmen; if I turn my back one minute, everything goes to hell. But I can fit you in tonight. Maybe I can give you some pointers on how to keep a job over a night cap at my place."

Slam!

The he-man, hero neighbor was afraid, too. He had spent his life playing strong and competent, afraid that someone might see how weak and unsure of himself he really felt.

"How dare she slam the door in my face!" he thought. "She had her chance and blew it," he muttered out loud, catching the ear of a middle-aged woman, standing helplessly by her car that had just run out of gas.

"Young man, thank heaven you came by just now. My car just stopped. I don't know what to do. I'm late for my doctor's appointment, and the car won't go."

"I'm in a hurry. Maybe your car needs service. When's the last time you had your oil changed? Let me check under your hood. This looks odd. Must be this whirlygig. Looks like the fan belt is loose. You probably burned up your engine. I could fix it, but I don't have time now. Where do you live?"

"A block that way. But it's such a long block, and I feel faint. Why do these things always happen to me? What can I do now? I don't know where to get the car fixed."

"You might have to get a new car. I only buy new cars. In the meantime, you ought to call a tow truck and get this heap off the road."

"Can't you call a tow truck for me? I don't know how. Besides, I feel faint. I *told* you I was on my way to the doctor."

This woman is afraid, as well. She is afraid to take responsibility for herself. She wants everyone else to take care of her. She has spent most of her life avoiding responsibility and can only present a litany of complaints—of what is wrong in her life and why she can do nothing to help herself.

Each of these people is a manipulator, but none of them is fully conscious of that fact. Their manipulative styles provide them with some measure of success: They are able to avoid what they fear, and they are often able to manipulate others to meet their needs, but their manipulative behaviors defeat their long-term personal goals and their relationships with others. The scenarios above are only slightly exaggerated. As psychologists, we meet people everyday who behave in one or more of these four styles.

The first man described above expresses phony love and caring to avoid what he fears: conflict and confrontation. His manipulative formula is "If I'm nice to everyone, avoid fights and anger, everyone will like me. I'll get what I want, and I won't get hurt." He can be described as a Nice Guy, and his behavior pattern is "pleasing and placating."

The young MBA graduate expresses phony anger because she is afraid of contact and intimacy. Her manipulative formula is "If I blame and attack others frequently, I can reject them before they reject me, and I won't get hurt." She is a Judge, and her predominant behavior pattern is "blaming and attacking."

The man in the third scenario expresses phony strength because he is afraid to be vulnerable. His manipulative formula is "If I am stronger than everyone else, no one can threaten me, and I won't get hurt." He is a Dictator, and his main behavior pattern is "controlling and dictating."

And the last woman described above expresses phony weakness because she is afraid that too much will be expected of her. Her manipulative formula is "If I am weak, others will have to help me, and I won't

Figure 2

The Manipulative Types

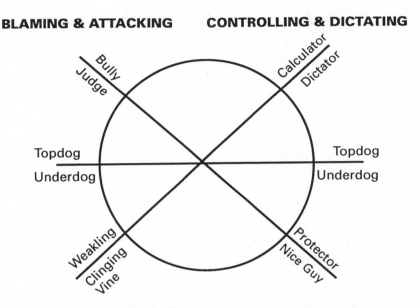

get hurt." She is a Weakling, and her primary pattern of behavior is to "avoid and withdraw."

In this book, although we are not abandoning the manipulative caricatures of Figure 1, we will be emphasizing manipulative *behavior* for several important reasons. The caricatures described above, such monikers as "dictator" and "weakling" and all their characteristics, have limitations in helping us to abandon manipulation. Indeed, they are devices useful to describe the intricacies of manipulation, the distinct patterns of manipulative relationships, and they help create awareness of the problem. But part of the problem of manipulators is that they see themselves and others in just such reductive terms.

To help manipulators abandon seeing themselves and others as "things," we prefer to emphasize manipulative behavior and action rather than to emphasize manipulative caricatures. If I say that I am a bully, I have no motivation to change—a bully is what I am. But if I say that I am *acting* like a bully, I can still be *me* as I change my bullying behavior.

Note that in Figure 2 the Judge and the Bully are described as *blaming* and *attacking*, the Dictator and the Calculator are described as *controlling* and *dictating*, the Weakling and the Clinging Vine are described as *avoiding* and *withdrawing*, and the Nice Guy and the Protector are described as *pleasing* and *placating*. These terms describe aspects of behavior, not what might be interpreted as the essence of the person.

Manipulators, whether they are functioning as "topdogs," commanding and authoritative, or as "underdogs," compliant and submissive, aren't purposely sabotaging their goals and relationships. They are coping, albeit in unsatisfactory and self-defeating ways.

The Basic Principles

As we said above, four basic conditions of every human's emotional experience lie on two polarities:

Love _____ Anger
Weakness _____ Strength

Love and anger are opposites, but are related to each other. Weakness and strength are also opposites, but relate to each other as well. These emotional elements of human experience are also the vehicles by which we express ourselves. But we can express ourselves with authentic love and anger or phony love and anger, with authentic strength and weakness or with phony strength and weakness. When we express our emotions truly, we are authentic. When we express them manipulatively, we are phony. We can recognize others' phoniness more readily than we can our own. One of the goals of this book is to help you to identify the manipulations you use. The other goal, equally important, is to help you to discover, as Kierkegaard said, "the Self that you truly are." Ironically, your true self is as difficult for you to see as is your manipulation. That authentic self you have been mistrusting, that core of your inner being, must be recognized and trusted to overcome your manipulation.

In this book, you'll see how, for some of you, manipulation is a way of life begun in early childhood and ingrained so deeply you can no longer distinguish the unreal mask you wear from your real face behind it. You'll have the chance to develop an awareness of yourself in the context of interpersonal relations, in learning about yourself and others simultaneously to maximize your potential as well as the potentials of other people in your life.

CHAPTER 2

The Problem

The modern human is a manipulator.

She is the computer salesperson, talking us into buying more "essential" extras than we could use in a lifetime, understand how to use in two, or pay for in three. He is the "responsible" parent, repeating the negative criticisms he heard as a child from his parents for the "benefit" of his own children. He is the minister, preaching in platitudes lest he offend important parishioners.

The realtor assures us that a particular piece of property will make our dreams come true. The politician promises everything except new taxes. The teenager assures her parents that the party planned in their home will not include booze or marijuana and that they should plan to spend the evening out. And even the aging parent embraces illness as a tool to manipulate the special attentions of busy sons and daughters.

The manipulator is legion. The manipulator is all of

us, consciously or unconsciously enjoying all the phony tricks learned between cradle and grave. In the process, we reduce ourselves and those around us into things to be controlled.

Not all of our manipulating is evil, of course. Some of it appears necessary in the competitive arena of earning a living. Much, however, is harmful since it masks real self-defeating tendencies that can explode into shattered lives, broken marriages, and ruined careers. Manipulation, we believe, is the "social sin" that separates us from one another in our marriages, alienates us from others at our jobs, and leaves us limping through life, handicapped with distorted selves.

The twentieth century has brought a deeper psychological understanding of the processes by which the modern manipulator has developed a personality resistant to growth and change. We know, for example, that manipulators lack the capacity to enjoy themselves, to use their knowledge, and to achieve a sense of aliveness and satisfaction. The manipulator's understanding of human nature becomes rigid; it focuses on the drive to control. To one degree or another this is true of everyone—you, us, the couple down the block, co-workers, friends, relatives.

Even toddling infants soon learn to drool or coo or cry with a vengeance on cue to get what they want—now! Little wonder then that the teenager, who is the most modern of modern people, feeling that life owes him or her a living and loving, refusing to meet life's challenge, astutely picks up subtle tactics of control and seduction. Teenagers find models everywhere: in real life, in movies, on television. Some tactics they learn from father, who stereotypically plays the controlling parent because he has a secret need for "omnipotence"; some from mother, who stereotypically manipulates with guilt-provoking statements to keep the teen "tied to her apron strings."

Manipulations are so much a part of our everyday life that the unskilled observer notices only the most blatant. They are like the birds that are all about us in the natural world. Do we actually identify or describe them?

While a particular plague of modern humans, manipulation is universal, endless and ageless. We read in the Old Testament in II Samuel, for instance, that David was so smitten with the beautiful wife of Uriah, that David gave orders for Uriah to be sent into the most dangerous part of the battle, where he would surely be slain and Bathsheba would be free. A gross manipulation. If we read further, we also see how David's latter days were tormented by his guilty love of the lady, and then how his handsome, rebellious son "stole the hearts of the men of Israel" and plotted to be king in his father's place. Yes, the ancients manipulated people for control and were themselves manipulated.

The paradox of modern humans is that they are intelligent beings with scientific knowledge of these things, yet they permit themselves to live in a state of low-grade vitality and unawareness. Generally, they do not suffer deeply, but how little they know of true creative living! Instead, manipulators behave as automatons.

Their world offers vast opportunities for enrichment and enjoyment, perhaps a wider scope than has ever been available before. Yet, they wander aimlessly, not really knowing what they want deep within, and are thereby unable to attain it.

They seem to feel that the time for fun, for pleasure, and for growing and learning is childhood and youth, and they abdicate life itself when they reach maturity. They go through a lot of motion, performing adult-ritualized procedures, like going to work, reading the paper, puttering around the house, walking through a mall—but the expressions on their faces indicate a lack of any real interest other than superficial attention to what is going on. Facial expressions seem limited to poker-faced, bored, aloof, or irritated. Above all, manipulators are complainers.

"Why isn't he ever on time?"

"Get out of my way, I'm in a hurry!"

"Why can't those kids behave?"

"What miserable weather!"

"Can't you do *anything* right?"

The rotten core of behavior—the part that is always there, but that nobody wants to admit to—is that manipulation is an attempt to get someone else to provide for you what you refuse to provide for yourself.

The best example is the manipulator's quest for happiness. Instead of saying, "What can *I* do for myself to develop my inner potentials, to expand the richness of my own personality, to tap my ability, to create pleasure and a sense of well-being?" the manipulator says, "If it weren't for you, I'd be happy. I'm bored and it's your fault. If you'd do what I told you to do, everything would be okay, and I'd be happy. If things were different, I'd be happy."

The bottom line is that manipulators cannot and will not be happy, ever, even if you sacrifice your mind, heart, and body for them because they will always be left with an empty and lonely person inside themselves. Blaming society, one's spouse, the job or the kids is only a smokescreen. Manipulators bore themselves with their impoverished beings. They frustrate themselves with their inner emptiness. They delude themselves with superficial role playing.

Manipulating one's world by playing certain roles is characteristic of the neurotic, of the underdeveloped, and of the immature. The hallmark of the modern manipulator is to be demanding rather than aware. No matter the manipulative style, manipulators are childishly demanding. The aggressive manipulator *demands*. The loving manipulator *cajoles*. The weakling manipulator *needs*. The strong manipulator *overpowers*.

Albert Ellis writes:

> It is an exceptionally clear-cut theory of personality disturbances—or human demandingness—that hypothesizes that people do not *get upset* but instead *upset themselves* by insisting that (a) they should be outstandingly loved and accomplished, (b) other people should be incredibly fair and giving, and (c) the world should be exceptionally easy and munificent.[1]

A manipulator is defined in psychological terms as "one who exploits, uses, and/or controls himself or herself and others, *as things*, in certain self-defeating ways." Manipulators undercut true spontaneity and the ability to express themselves directly and creatively. They are numb automatons, wasting hours trying to recapture the past or ensure the future. They talk about their feelings but are rarely in vital contact with them. In fact, they are quite glib about their troubles but generally quite inept at coping with them. Manipulators grope along under a sea of masks and concealments, unaware of the real richness of being.

An actualizer, by contrast, may be defined as a person who appreciates and trusts himself or herself and others, learns from the past and plans for the future but *lives in the present.* Actualizers, having a keen awareness of their feelings and accurate perceptions of their surroundings, experience and express their emotions in *congruence* with their circumstances. They do not have "hidden agendas" behind their expressions of love, for example. And when they express anger, there is an obvious reason for it. Actualizers, being accurate perceivers, have trust in their own capabilities and the abilities of others and do not have unrealistic or unreasonable expectations of either. Liking themselves, they are able to notice and appreciate the likability of others. They are more cooperative than competitive, more appreciative than critical, and experience joy in their work and creativity in their play. Actualizers are problem solvers more than problem reciters. They are unencumbered by masks of deception, and "what you see is what you get."

The paradox is that each of us is partly a manipulator and partly an actualizer. The goal, of course, is to tip the scale to the side of the actualizer.

A person who is actualizing listens to his or her feelings, communicates needs and preferences, admits to faults or misbehaviors, offers real help when needed, can be honestly and constructively assertive, and is preeminently a person of open mind and responsive heart.

The manipulator, on the other hand, habitually conceals and camouflages real feelings behind a repertoire of behavior that runs the scale from servile flattery to arrogant hostility to withdrawn snobbishness in the continuous campaign to serve his or her own wishes or unconscious needs.

We believe that most manipulators aren't totally aware of the compulsive and defeating nature of their approaches to life. If confronted, they will respond defensively with "That's just the way I am" or "How dare you say that." The first step toward actualizing is to entertain the possibility that you are a manipulator and to embrace the idea that you can change.

But *change* may not be the best word to describe what we mean about actualizing. It isn't like changing the tire on your car or changing into new clothes. Your *self* is not an external thing to be owned, used, and discarded for a better model. Your self is what you are, not what you have. You are not a thing, but a being.

Manipulation, at its worst, is an expression of lost trust in the vitality of the real self (the *core* self, of which we shall speak later) and of the subsequent need to compulsively *over control* one's own personality and one's ongoing interactions with others.

The myriad ways human beings manipulate themselves and one another can be reduced by modern psychological theory to four major patterns. We manipulate ourselves and others by habitually acting overly

- nice (we mainly express love)
- aggressive (we mainly express anger)
- helpless (we mainly express weakness)
- pompous (we mainly express strength).

When we express one emotion predominantly, the emotion is not always appropriate to the situation.

Our emotions become habits to meet our "secret agendas" and are, therefore, not genuine. By expressing one emotion predominantly, we also deny the opposite, equally important, part of ourselves that contributes to our wholeness. A polarity, two opposing things connected on a continuum—such as day and night and every second of every hour between midnight and noon—is needed for the "whole."

Therefore, the polar opposites of love on one end and anger on the other, weakness on one end and strength on the other, are necessary for human "wholeness." Psychological health of the personality is attained by integrating and coordinating the polarities of *love* and *anger*, *strength* and *weakness*, in the service of the *actualizing core* (see Fig. 3). Without this integration, the personality (the healthy core) is fragmented, at war with itself. Through the eyes of such a fragmented personality, the world is a battleground and others are enemies. It is the world of the topdog and the underdog.

NOTE

1. Albert Ellis, *Humanistic Psychotherapy: The Rational Emotive Approach* (New York, The Julian Press, 1973), p. 15.

Figure 3

Polar "LAWS" of Personality

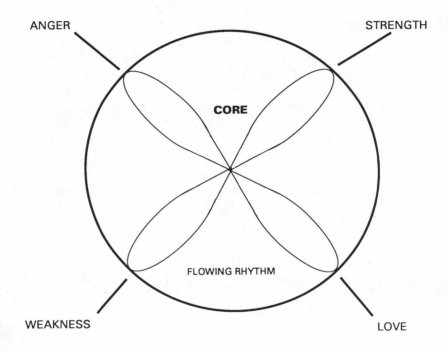

CHAPTER 3

Topdog vs. Underdog

Picture this scene: An African plain lies in the distance. It is peaceful, and a herd of kudu is grazing in the twilight. Suddenly a young buck enters the herd, challenging the leader. A fight ensues. Nearby a lioness is stalking a few stragglers from the herd intent on killing one to provide food for herself and her cubs.

And picture this scene: It is morning rush hour in Manhattan. Nothing is peaceful in the blare of horns, roar of traffic and shouts of frustration. A city bus, by virtue of its size, manages to cut in front of an ordinarily aggressive taxi driver, who yells in impotent rage at the indifferent bus driver. Above the city in a luxury penthouse, several children are playing on the terrace in a sandbox. One of them has just wrested a particularly prized toy from another child. Loud screaming ensues. The babysitter, observing the incident, returns the toy to the crying toddler, who whimpers in satisfaction.

It seems that the world is filled with struggle and

that "might makes right." It seems that the bigger, the stronger, the more powerful rule. Even the forces of nature—hurricanes, tornadoes, oppressive heat, drought—are humbling experiences to humans who seem helpless against such power. Nations with great military arsenals seem impervious to threats from countries with less military might. Wealthy individuals control and direct. Impoverished individuals accept and endure. Big adults make the rules. Little children obey them. It is a world of the strong and the weak—the topdogs and the underdogs.

Experience has shown, however, that in the face of the destructive forces of nature, humans prepare, adapt, and survive. Nations with great military arsenals have fallen to weaker nations whom they have oppressed. Wealthy individuals are often controlled and directed by the responsibilities their positions impose. Impoverished individuals are able to transform their conditions. And, everyday, little children subvert the rules their parents make.

One of the characteristics of humans is that they can adapt to their environment, a trait that partially accounts for the survival and development of our species. Socialization, or the formation of groups of individuals who agree to work together to promote the safety and prosperity of each member, attests to human initiative and adaptibility. On a global level, nations of individuals agree to common goals among themselves and negotiate agreements with other nations of individuals. On the world scene, however, the dance continues between the topdogs and the underdogs, the strong and the weak—macro-manipulation interspersed here and there, now and then, with impulses of a higher nature, which is called civilization.

Wherever two individuals are in interaction, the same dance is performed. Frederick Perls, who first used the terms *topdog* and *underdog* in a psychological sense, used the terms to describe not only two persons in interaction, but also two parts of a personality. He said:

> The topdog usually is righteous and authoritarian; he knows best. He is sometimes right, but always righteous. The topdog is a bully, and works with "You should" and "You should not." The topdog manipulates with demands and threats of catastrophe, such as, "If you don't, then—you won't be loved, you won't get to heaven, you will die," and so on.
>
> The underdog manipulates with being defensive, apologetic, wheedling, playing the cry-baby, and such. The underdog has no power. The underdog is the Mickey Mouse. The topdog is the Super Mouse. And the underdog works like this: "Mañana." "I try my best." "Look, I try again and again; I can't help it if I fail." "I can't help it if I forgot your birthday." "I have such good intentions." So you see the underdog is cunning, and usually gets the better of the topdog because the underdog is not as primitive as the topdog. So the topdog and underdog strive for control. Like every parent and child, they strive with each other for control. The person is fragmented into controller and controlled. This inner conflict, the struggle between the topdog and the underdog, is never complete, because topdog as well as underdog fight for their lives.[1]

Understanding these elements of human interaction, the topdogs against the underdogs, and the techniques each uses in trying to survive and prevail provides a model of our own inner world. The topdog in us accounts for our perfectionism, our expectations of ourselves and others that can never be satisfied. And the underdog in us accounts for our rationalizations and our abdication of responsibility.

Have you ever played the "Self-torture Game"? That is what Perls calls the inner war between topdog and underdog. He describes it like this: "The other day I had a talk with a friend of mine and I told her, 'Please get into your nut: mistakes are not sins,' and she wasn't half as relieved as I thought she would be. Then I realized, if mistakes are not a sin any more, how can she castigate others who make mistakes?"[2]

The topdog perfectionist in us, who must judge and criticize others, must in all fairness apply the same rules to itself. And the underdog, helpless one in us, who cowers at the self-flaggelation, retreats to "I tried. I cannot help it if I'm not perfect."

The topdogs who want others to see how important they are ("I'm the supervisor of this office, and I know best what to do and how to do it") at the same time, when confronted with a real challenge, quake with the fear that they will not be able to handle it. A review of the characteristics of these warring factions might seem vaguely familiar.

A client of ours has been keeping a daily journal of his experiences and feelings, which documents his personal topdog/underdog battle (the topdog voice is in bold print):

"I can't stand myself for my anger. I once saw a repressive sign on a desk that said,

**'Keep your temper, no one else wants it.'
That's exactly how I feel about myself right
now."**
"My problem is that my awful thinking
always seeks to snatch defeat from the jaws
of victory. It's almost like I'm afraid to win
anything. I feel more comfortable in defeat."
"Mom always taught me not to fight, so I
gathered from that that if I left others alone
they'd do the same for me. I didn't know all
these aggressive people existed out there."
**"If I'm going to buck up to these people, I
need to be firm and stay that way."**
"I'm afraid I'll say too little, yet afraid I'll
say too much."
**"These people have horrible, obnoxious
faults, and they're not hidden, but written on
their faces. That's why I clash with them."**
"I feel terrible about myself. **It proves to
me that I'm a terrible person** for all this
verbal violence and that people can't stand
me."

The concept of the internal topdog and underdog is
essential to understanding the mechanics of manipulation and to finding ways to overcome the lengthy,
dead-end dialogues we have with ourselves. Do not
confuse such a self-dialogue with the conscience. The
voice of the conscience is direct, constructive, and
wise. The voice of the topdog/underdog manipulator is
indirect, convoluted, and destructive.

Our client's journal shows a tortuous battle between his topdog and his underdog. His topdog
exaggerates his expectations of others—they must be

faultless and totally amenable to his needs—so he blames and attacks others for their shortcomings on both counts. Then his underdog emerges—he must be careful, or the others might blame and attack him—and he retreats into his weakling role of avoiding and withdrawing, whereupon his topdog flogs him for his own imperfection. He *should* have been able to stand up to the others without yelling and making a fool of himself. He *should* have been able to assert his own rights. He *shouldn't* have been such a weakling. He *should* be perfect.

While his topdog is *shoulding* him, his underdog is berating him for hurting others' feelings, recommending that it would have been safer had he played the "injured party" role. "Next time, lay a little guilt on the guy. Then clam up and let him wonder what's wrong," his underdog counsels.

As Perls says, the battle between the internal topdog and the underdog in the manipulator is one unto death—the death of self-esteem and happy, productive relationships.

INTEGRATING YOUR TOPDOG AND UNDERDOG

One way to integrate your topdog and underdog is to accept the paradox that both exist in you *and they are equal*, like a two-party system in politics or a battery with positive and negative poles. A democracy collapses without opposing, equally strong political parties. A battery will not work without the positive and negative electrical charges, and a healthy human being cannot function at the fully human level without both strength and weakness, love and anger.

A simple example from a therapy session with a woman who feels lonely illustrates:

Therapist: Be your lonesome self, weak.
Client: *I feel so blue and unhappy. I need a friend. (Underdog)*
Therapist: Now be your opposite self, strong.
Client: *I can be my own friend. I don't need anybody else. (Topdog)*
Therapist: Now be the weak one again.
Client: *I'm not enough. I need others. (Underdog)*
Therapist: Now be the strong one and answer.
Client: *I am enough, but I can see that having a friend would be good. (TOPDOG/underdog)*
Therapist: Be weak again.
Client: *Ok. I may not always feel that I am "enough," but I'll admit that I might be. (UNDERDOG/topdog)*
Therapist: Be strong and weak.
Client: *I am "enough" and I can be a friend not only to myself but also to another. Then I guess I'll have two friends. (TOPDOG/UNDERDOG)*

The above is an example of an individual *listening* to both sides, both her weak underdog and her strong topdog. By accepting and listening to both sides of herself, the antagonistic poles become complementary. When both sides of ourselves are accepted equally, the power of integration occurs.

Another way to integrate your topdog and underdog is to express your feelings as accurately as possible. A young woman, recently married, illustrates:

Therapist: Tell me how you feel when John flirts, as you put it, with other women?

Client: *It doesn't really bother me that much. (Underdog)*

Therapist: But you notice it. What do you feel?

Client: *It's irritating when he interrupts our conversation to tell some waitress how terrific she looks. (Topdog)*

Therapist: Do you tell him?

Client: *No. I don't want to ruin our marriage with jealousy. I love him. (Underdog)*

Therapist: Do you feel loving at those times?

Client: *Not really. I guess I feel inadequate. (Underdog)*

Therapist: Are you inadequate?

Client: *No. (Topdog)*

Therapist: What are you, then?

Client: *I guess I'm damn mad at him. It really hurts to be treated that way. (TOPDOG/UNDERDOG)*

The closer the woman came to accurately expressing her feelings, the more she was able to: (1) integrate her topdog (anger) with her underdog (love), and (2) resolve the dichotomy that was robbing her of her self-esteem and falsifying her communications.

As Maslow says, in healthier people dichotomies are resolved and polarities disappear.[3] Learning to listen to both your topdog and underdog—giving them equal time, so to speak, and learning to accurately express your feelings—telling the truth, enables you to integrate your warring factions and transcend your manipulations.

NOTES

1. Frederick Perls, *Gestalt Therapy Verbatim* (Lafayette, Calif.: Real People Press, 1969), p. 18.
2. Ibid.
3. See Abraham Maslow, *Motivation and Personality* (New York: Harper and Bros. 1954), p. 233.

CHAPTER 4

The Manipulators

We believe that the modern manipulator has developed from our "scientific" emphases as well as from our marketplace orientation, which sees humans as things to know about, to influence, and to manipulate. Witness the presidential campaigns or any major election to see how the electorate is analyzed and fed images designed to influence their votes based on the opinion polls. The candidates are frequently advised not to reveal too much of their true selves, but to display themselves as metaphors of whatever the current poll indicates will satisfy public opinion—a televised visit to a family farm, a picture of the candidate hugging an elderly person at a retirement community. Wearing a hard hat. A military helmet. A baseball cap. A thing.

Erich Fromm has said that *things* can be dissected or manipulated without damage to their natures, but a human being is not a *thing*.[1] People cannot be dissected without being destroyed; they cannot be manipulated without being harmed. Yet, the very objective of the marketplace is to achieve this "thingness" in people!

In the marketplace, people are no longer persons but customers. To the sales manager, they are prospects; to the tailor they are suits; to the bond salesman they are bank accounts. Even at hair salons, where a rather intimate service is performed, the customer is a tipper. All of this tends to depersonalize us and deprive us of our individuality, and we resent it. We all want particularity, but that is not what we have when we're hooked into our commercial world, where the quality of individuality is destroyed. When the con artists of the selling game cajole us with stock phrases, meaning not a bit of it, we resent it and them.

We are all in the same boat. We all have the manipulative potentials we have come to resent in others. We have at our disposal a variety of manipulative actions and intentions. Sometimes we are "avoiding and withdrawing." Sometimes "blaming and attacking." Sometimes "pleasing and placating." We seem different to different people. We employ certain manipulations to some people and different manipulations to others. This is the reason that we cannot judge someone by another's opinion. Too often, another's opinion of someone is based on having seen only certain sides of that person.

CAUSES OF MANIPULATION

The causes of manipulation are many.

We would agree with Fredrick Perls that one cause of manipulation lies in the human's eternal conflict between self-support and environmental support.

There is a good deal of this conflict in employer-employee relationships. Often an employee, even when given the authority to make decisions and to take action, cannot do so. Unable to trust his or her own ability to know general company policy and to adapt it to changing situations, the employee defers decisions to higher-ups or to so-called authorities. Such an employee refuses to depend on self-support, but must look to authorities—environmental support.

On the other hand, many employers refuse to trust the individual abilities of their employees. A salesman, for example, may be treated like a machine, whose sole function is to perform within the limited framework of the employer's sales manual. This "sales machine," robbed of personality, treats the customer in the same depersonalized manner.

Not trusting oneself for support, a manipulator tends to believe that salvation lies in the hands of others. Yet, not trusting others completely, he or she manipulates the other in an effort to have that support. The manipulator rides the coattail of the other person and then attempts to steer him or her. Refusing to drive himself or herself, the manipulator *drives the driver*.

The operative word here is *distrust*. We do not trust the natural organismic balance each of us has, which would allow us to live our lives simply and feelingly. Married couples often form a complex manipulative partnership to cope with their distrust of self-sufficiency and of others. For example, a husband with a penchant for withdrawing and avoiding uses his wife, who has an inclination for blaming and attacking, as his "mouthpiece." It is the perfect solution for the husband, who feels he is insufficient to confront others about his needs. He lets his wife convey his demands to others. Such an arrangement is a safe haven for a withdrawing and avoiding husband. His wife is on the front line, and if his demand elicits a negative or hostile response from the other, she gets the heat. And, of course, he can resort to blaming and attacking her when his manipulation has failed. It was *her* fault.

Erich Fromm has suggested a second cause for manipulation. He reasons that the ultimate relationship between two humans is that of love and that love is knowing a human being as he or she is and loving his or her ultimate essence.[2] We believe that this desire to love and be loved is a wonderfully healthy, innately human experience, but our manipulative inclinations *to be lovable* and *to make lovable* are the sabotaging elements. If loving is knowing a human being as he or she is, we fear that we are not very lovable as we truly are, and the other person is not very lovable as he or she truly is. So we begin masking and costuming ourselves in an effort to make ourselves lovable, and we begin our attempts to change and mold others to meet our expectations of what is lovable in them.

The world's great religions teach us to love our neighbor as we love ourselves, but here, unfortunately, we run into an operational snag. How many of us know how to love ourselves? Most aren't even aware that we can't love our neighbor *until we love ourselves*. We seem to assume that the more perfect we appear, the more flawless, the more we will be loved. Actually, the reverse is more apt to be true. The more willing we are to admit our weaknesses as human beings, the more lovable we are. Nevertheless, love is an achievement not easy to attain, thus the alternative that the manipulator has is a desperate one: that of complete power over the other person, the power that makes others do what *we* want, feel what *we* want, and think what *we* want, and that transforms others into things, *our* things.

A third possible cause of manipulation is posed by James Bugental and the existentialists. They point out that risk and contingency surround us, as though our every act were a stone dropped in a pond. The number of risks and potential outcomes are beyond our knowing. Humans feel powerless. According to Bugental, the *underdog manipulator's* response is, "'Since I can't control everything that will determine what happens to me, I have no control at all.' Experiencing the unpredictability of his life, the patient gives up and enacts this feeling of having no possibility of affecting what happens to him. He makes himself totally an object."[3]

The *topdog manipulator*, on the other hand, "victimizes other people, capitalizing on their powerlessness. Parents who are oppressed by the dread of powerlessness often need to make their children excessively dependent upon them and to defeat the child's efforts to gain independence."[4] Usually the parent is the topdog and the child the underdog, and we see the use of the "*If* you eat your potatoes, *then* you may watch television." "*If* you do your homework, *then* you may use the car." Naturally, the child soon learns the technique, too: "If I mow the lawn, then how much do I get?" "If Jim's father lets him use the car every weekend, then why won't you?"

The truly topdog manipulator might simply roar: "Do as I say and no questions." We see it in business: "I own 51 percent of the stock, and they will work on

Saturdays because *I* want them to." Even in education the founder of a certain college used to say: "I don't care what color the buildings are, so long as they are blue."

A fourth cause of manipulation is suggested in the writings of Jay Haley, Eric Berne, and William Glasser. Haley, in his work with schizophrenics, found that the schizophrenic is intensely afraid of *close* interpersonal relationships and so tries to avoid them. Berne suggests that people play games to regulate their emotions and thereby avoid *intimacy*. Glasser suggests that one of our basic fears is the fear of involvement. In effect, then, a manipulator is a person who ritualistically relates to people in an effort to avoid intimacy or involvement.

A fifth suggested cause for manipulation comes from the work of Albert Ellis. He writes that each of us learns certain illogical assumptions about living. One of them is the dire necessity to be approved by *everyone*. Underdog manipulators, Ellis suggests, are persons who refuse to be truthful and honest with others and instead try to please everyone because they foolishly believe that they must gain everyone's approval.[5]

We believe that these five possible causes of manipulation can be summarized in this way: People manipulate because they are afraid.

NOTES

1. See Erich Fromm, "Man Is Not a Thing," *Saturday Review* (March 16, 1957): 9-11.
2. Ibid.
3. J. F. T. Bugental, *The Search for Authenticity* (New York: Holt, Rinehard & Winston, 1965), p. 298.
4. Ibid., p. 299.
5. Albert Ellis, "New Approaches to Psychotherapy," *Journal of Clinical Psychology. Monograph Supplement* (1955): 11.

CHAPTER 5

The Actualizers

What is actualization?

In a way, the term *actualization* (to make or become real) is another chapter in the history of the human endeavor to define what constitutes a good life, what it is to have a life well-lived. A great body of writings, from antiquity to the present, documents the human impulse to know what makes life good, meaningful, and, therefore, worthwhile.

In the Bible, we find Christ telling us, "I have come that they may have life, and that they may have it more abundantly" (John 10:10 NKJV). Indeed, the Bible is rich with commentary about what makes a worthwhile life. Classical drama and the Greek philosophers addressed the nature of humankind in terms of meaning and potential. The great literature of the Renaissance included many work of this nature, such as *The Courtier* by Castiglione, *The Governor* by Sir Thomas Elyot, and *Utopia* by Sir Thomas More.

The writings of Confucius are an example of the same impulse in the Eastern culture.

The common threads in all of these writings are what enriches an *individual* life (intrapersonal), how an individual contributes to the common good (interpersonal) and what is the human place in eternity (spiritual and conceptual).

Sigmund Freud, the founder of psychoanalysis, in a sense, is a part of this tradition, but his studies and writings emphasize the darker side of the human being. His concern is with what makes a human life "bad." He studied the human as being diseased, and his revolutionary concept has influenced nearly every aspect of our culture and has confined much of psychology to a medical model.

Reacting against the Freudian emphasis on disease and returning to the larger tradition as described above, Abraham Maslow studied healthy humans and discovered the concept of "self-actualization." Whereas many psychologists, following Freud's medical model, believed that we could understand psychological health by first understanding psychological illness, Maslow suggested the alternative viewpoint. He taught that we can understand psychological health by studying the lives of people who have achieved a high degree of interpersonal satisfaction and self-fulfillment, the healthy champions. It is largely from his research that we draw our understanding of these people.

The persons he studied included acquaintances, friends, and such public and historical figures as Lincoln, Jefferson, Einstein, Eleanor Roosevelt, Jane Addams, Schweitzer, G. W. Carver, and Henry David Thoreau. Although these individuals cannot be described as perfect by any standard (no human is), their lives and the qualities that informed them, as discovered and defined by Maslow, provide valuable guidelines to us. In general, he said:

> By definition, self-actualizing people are gratified in all their basic needs. . . . They have a feeling of belongingness and rootedness, they are satisfied in their love needs, have friends and feel loved and loveworthy, they have status and place in life and respect from other people, and they have a reasonable feeling of worth and self-respect.[1]

His study discloses the fact that self-actualizing persons whose basic needs are satisfied have additional motivations of an even higher nature. Some are conceptual:

- they delight in bringing about justice;
- they try to set things right, to clean up bad situations;
- they manage somehow simultaneously to love the world as it is and to try to improve it;
- in all cases [studied] it was as if they could see both good and evil realistically.[2]

Some higher motivations are interpersonal:

- they do not *need* to be loved by everyone;
- they like to reward and praise promise, talent, virtue;
- [they have] great pleasure in their children and in helping them grow into good adults.[3]

Some are intrapersonal:

- they love doing things well, "doing a good job";
- they enjoy taking on responsibilities (that they can

handle well); and certainly don't fear or evade their responsibilities.[4]

Even though a mere 1 percent of the population, by Maslow's reckoning, is fully self-actualized, knowing of real people with these qualities furnishes the rest of us with models for emulation. Such models are necessary precursors to change because they help us to form the "idea" of a new, manipulation-freer life. Unless we can concretely envision ourselves "being real," we are stuck with our old masks and deceptions.

Being real has a great deal to do with appreciating our own uniqueness, as Martin Buber expresses it in his book *The Way of Man:*

> Every person born into this world represents something new, something that never existed before, something original and unique. "It is the duty of every person . . . to know and consider that he is unique in the world in his particular character and that there has never been anyone like him in the world . . ." Every man's foremost task is the actualization of his unique, unprecedented and never recurring potentialities, and not the repetition of something that another, and be it even the greatest, has already achieved.[5]

Maslow's "healthy champions" seem to understand their singularity in the world, as described by Buber, but they also have many common characteristics. In the film *Maslow and Self-Actualization* and in his books, he describes some of their common traits.

SENSE OF HUMOR

Self-actualized people have a different sense of humor from the ordinary type. It is not hostile. It is not at someone else's expense. It focuses more on the foolishness of the human situation. Their humor is usually thought-provoking, and many times they are able to laugh at themselves. Lincoln's humor, for example, was very much in this vein. He told one story that many believed could have applied to himself.

It seems that a woman on horseback on a narrow trail came upon a man on a horse. She stopped her horse, looked the man over, and blurted out, "Well, for the land's sake, you are the homeliest man I ever saw!" The man replied, "Yes ma'am, but I can't help that." "No, I suppose not," she replied, "but you might stay at home."[6]

Here is another story Lincoln told, perhaps, to point out that common sense has a wisdom that transcends logic: "If three pigeons sit on a fence and you shoot and kill one of them, how many will be left?" Lincoln asked. The answer was, "Two, of course." To which he responded, "No, there won't, for the other two will fly away."[7]

Social Interest

Maslow's "healthy champions" all had some unselfish involvement with others. They behaved as though each member of the human race were a personal family member, worthy of affection in spite of the way each person may act. But the self-actualizers also could express "righteous indignation" toward cruelty, hypocrisy, or phoniness in others.

Interpersonal Relations

They tend to have deeper and more meaningful interpersonal relations than the average adult—close relationships with a few, rather than superficial relationships with many. These people are more able to be nondemanding and noninterfering with those they love, delighting in the loved ones for themselves, not for what the loved ones can provide in return—love without guile, design, or calculation of any selfish kind.[8]

Maslow called this kind of love *being love*. Such a love, he said, "makes for less abstracting, less viewing of less-than-the whole, less atomizing or dissecting . . . structuring, organizing, shaping, molding. . ." of the loved one, and the object of such love "remains more whole, more unified, which amounts to saying more itself."[9] A "being" lover sees more easily the nature of the loved one in his or her own right and in his or her own style of being.

The opposite of being love Maslow called *deficiency love*, which is a manipulative kind of love. Manipulative lovers like to dissect the loved ones to discover and declare their faults as a means of gaining control over the loved ones. They like to mold and recreate the loved ones. Manipulators love because they feel a sense of lacking something in themselves, and they expect the loved one to fill their personal void. Their love is absolutely conditional and can be withdrawn if the loved one fails to provide all the demands.

Awareness

Actualized people, Maslow's research found, have a more efficient perception of reality than do others. They can see or perceive others intuitively and correctly. They cannot be conned. They don't come into situations with preconceptions, but seem able to leap to right conclusions. They also have a freshness of appreciation, and their senses are not dulled by seemingly common, everyday experiences. They experience joy in the miracles of everyday life that the rest of us hardly see, hear, or feel—a baby's smile, a loving glance, a cooling breeze, a heartfelt compliment, a warm bed, a sunset, a lovely person's profile.

Mission

Each of Maslow's subjects had some life task to fulfill that enlisted much of his or her time and energy. It was as if each of them had found and recognized some specific purpose to their being in the world that they pursued with great persistence. To paraphrase the famous line from John F. Kennedy's inaugural address, they did not ask what the world could do for them, but what they could do for the world. The "world," to a self-actualized person, could be as large as just that—the world—or as small as a neighborhood or family.

Autonomy

The subjects of Maslow's study depended on their own potentialities and latent resources, rather than on others, for their continued growth. Their sense of self and their stability can be described, Maslow said, as "self-contained." This independence of the physical and social environment accounted for their serenity in the face of deprivations, frustrations, and set-backs that might drive others to the brink of suicide. They did not depend on others' love and respect for their own development. Their ability to get to such a point of independence, however, was largely made possible because they had received in the past love and respect from others.[10]

Acceptance

Self-actualized people are accepting of the real nature of themselves and others. Maslow said that just as "one does not complain about water because it is wet, or about rocks because they are hard," a self-actualized person does not complain about human nature in himself or in others.[11]" Healthy people do not feel guilt, shame, sadness, anxiety, or defensiveness about things that are part of their nature as humans. They don't say to themselves, "I am so ashamed that I'm so short" or "I wouldn't want to be seen with her; she's not very attractive." Healthy people do feel guilty about improvable shortcomings, such as laziness, jealousy, prejudice, and hurting others.[12]

What makes healthy people feel bad are the discrepancies between what is and what might be, not in the inherent nature of things or persons, but in the conditions or situations that might be changed or improved.

In truth, we cannot change ourselves. We can find ourselves and develop what we find. That is what actualization is—becoming our real selves. That is easy to say, but how does it happen? How do we know who we really are? What is a *self*, anyway?

You may have not thought of it, but the concept of self can vary from person to person. **Some of us think of self primarily in terms of the physical:**

- size and shape,
- color of skin, hair, and eyes,
- our attractiveness or unattractiveness;

in terms of sensations:
- hungry or full,
- in pain or in pleasure,
- well or sick,
- tired or energetic;

in terms of feelings:
- bored or interested,
- happy or sad,
- angry or loving.

Others think of self primarily in terms of work or primary occupation:
- a professor,
- a truck driver,
- a parent,
- a counselor.

And still others think of self conceptually:
- good or bad,
- kind or cruel,
- smart or stupid,
- friendly or surly,
- accepted or misunderstood.

We can see ourselves as if in a vacuum—alone with no connection to our environment and others; as an outline totally defined by a background of our environment and others; or as a being who is partially defined by our environment and others and partially defining our environment and others.

Rollo May said that "consciousness of one's self is

always a unique act—I can never know exactly how you see yourself and you never can know exactly how I relate to myself. This is the inner sanctum where each man must stand alone," and where we must find the strength to stand as individuals and, through our own affirmation and choice, learn to love each other.[13]

Developing a strong sense of self is a prerequisite to actualization, and it requires a leap of faith. You do not have to prove your self-worth; you may assume it. As an acorn does not have to prove it has the potential to become a tree before it can grow, a human does not have to prove his or her own unique self-hood to realize it.

A way to begin to discover your unique self is to keep a daily journal entitled "This Is Me." Each day, write a description of yourself, a one-line entry, or several pages. Be sure to describe yourself in terms of your thoughts, feelings, bodily sensations, actions, and experiences alone and with others. You may be surprised at how much you discover about yourself and how the horizons of yourself begin to widen. Unlike the acorn, which can become only a tree, the range of what you are is far less limited. As a person, a unique individual, you have freedom, choice, and responsibility. As a manipulator, you abdicate all three.

NOTES

1. Abraham Maslow, *The Farther Reaches of Human Nature* (New York: The Viking Press, 1971), p. 299.
2. Ibid., pp. 308-9.
3. Ibid.
4. Ibid.
5. Martin Buber, *The Way of Man* (Chicago: Wilcox and Follett, 1951), p. 16.

6. Carl Sandburg, *Abraham Lincoln: The Prairie Years*, vol. 2 (New York: Harcourt, Brace & World, 1926), pp. 77-78.
7. Ibid, p. 79.
8. Maslow, *The Farther Reaches of Human Nature*, p. 13.
9. Ibid.
10. Abraham Maslow, *Motivation and Personality* (New York: Harper and Bros., 1954), p. 214.
11. Ibid, p. 207.
12. Ibid, p. 208.
13. Rollo May, *Man's Search for Himself* (New York: W. W. Norton, 1953), pp. 94-95.

CHAPTER 6

Manipulators and Actualizers Contrasted

A manipulator's life involves four fundamental characteristics: deception, unawareness, control, and cynicism. The actualizer's life is marked by four opposing characteristics: honesty, awareness, freedom, and trust.

MANIPULATORS	ACTUALIZERS
1. *Deception* (phoniness). Manipulators use tricks, techniques, and maneuvers. They put on an act, and play roles to create an *impression*. Their expressed feelings are deliberately chosen to fit a "secret agenda."	1. *Honesty* (authenticity). Actualizers are able to be and to express their feelings, whatever they may be. There is a congruence between an actualizer's feelings and expressions, actions and situations.
2. **Unawareness** (limited, selective vision). Manip-	2. **Awareness** (accurate perception, appropriate re-

59

ulators miss meaning and significance in experience, have "tunnel vision"—see only what they wish to see, hear only what they wish to hear.

3. **Control** (closed, deliberate). Manipulators play life like a chess game. They appear relaxed, yet are controlled and controlling, concealing their motives from "opponents."

4. **Cynicism** (distrust). Manipulators basically distrust themselves and others. Down deep they don't trust human nature. They see relationships as having only two alternatives: to control or to be controlled.

sponses). Actualizers fully see and listen to themselves and others. They find meaning and significance in life experience.

3. **Freedom** (spontaneity, openness). Actualizers are spontaneous. They have the freedom to be and to express their potentials. They are masters of life rather than puppets, subjects rather than objects.

4. **Trust** (faith, belief). Actualizers have a deep trust in themselves and others. They can relate to and cope with life in the here and now.

Humans have many actualizing potentials. Some we come to appreciate or value more than others. The more we can appreciate all aspects of ourselves, the more fully actualizing we become. We can be angry at times, loving at others, strong sometimes and weak sometimes.

But as manipulators, each aspect of ourselves that we disvalue becomes an act of disowning a part of ourselves. And what we disown, we must treat as "things." When we do something we dislike, we say,

"That's not like me!" *"It* came over me," instead of *"I* regret that *I* did that" or *"I'm* sorry *I* said that." Soon this tendency to disown or to deny our*selves* spreads into all areas of our lives. When the home team is losing, it is no longer "our team" but "that team." Similarly, one's spouse becomes a "nag," a "ball and chain," a "meal ticket." When you feel like an "it," others about you seem like "its" too. As actualizers, we appreciate ourselves and others and don't need to manipulate others to control them. We operate from a position of *self worth* rather than from a position of *deficiency.*

The manipulator, always assuming a deficiency in self and others, is compelled to fight. Life is a battle with strategy, tactics, tricks, or games necessary for survival. When a manipulator loses a battle or contest, he or she feels that everything is lost. The actualizer, assuming sufficiency in self and others and not hampered by the manipulator's battle gear, sees life as an endless array of exciting opportunities to learn and to grow and to share.

Here we must make what is perhaps the most important statement of this book: ***While the manipulator is a many-faceted person of antagonistic opposites, the actualizer is a many-faceted person of complementary opposites.***

Figure 4 shows the actualizing person as a combination of four complementary potentials, all developed out of former manipulative potentials.

1. *From Dictator to Leader.* The leader guides and serves rather than controls and dictates. The leader is forceful and decisive, yet not domineering and arbitrary.

The complementary opposite to the leader is the empathizer. The empathizer not only talks, but also listens and is aware of his or her weaknesses. Although the empathizer has high expectations of self and others, he or she can understand and accept human fallibility.

The actualizer integrates his or her leadership and empathy. The qualities of leadership and empathy are dependent upon each other. Without empathy, a leader is more likely to be a dictator; without leadership, the quality of empathy may be hollow.

2. *From Calculator to Respecter.* The respecter, rather than using or exploiting others, creatively participates in cooperative endeavors with others. The respecter, trusting and respecting the qualities of self and others, is able to bring out the best in both.

The complementary opposite of the respecter is the appreciator. The appreciator is able to celebrate and admire the talents of others without envy. He or she can tolerate differences in others and does not *need* to have others to think, believe, and behave the same as he or she thinks, believes, and behaves.

The actualizer integrates his or her respect and appreciation. A respecter without appreciation is a calculator. Appreciation without the creativity and cooperation of a respecter is like a birthday card bought but never given.

3. *From Bully to Assertor.* The assertor, confident of his or her rights and strength, is direct and straightforward. Assertors do not view others as enemies to be vanquished, but are also not afraid to stand up and be counted.

The complementary opposite of the assertor is the

Figure 4

The Actualizing Types
Complementary Opposites

TOP DOG

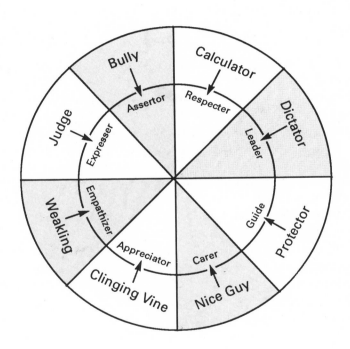

UNDERDOG

carer. The carer is not the obsequious Nice Guy, but is affectionate and friendly.

The actualizer integrates his or her assertion and caring. An assertor without caring is a bully. And a carer who will not assert his or her needs is just playing the "martyr" role.

4. *From Judge to Expresser.* The expresser is not judgmental of others, but is able to express his or her convictions strongly and well.

The complementary opposite of the expressor is the guide. The guide does not presume to protect and teach others, but willingly encourages others onto the path of understanding. A guide, knowing that each person must find his or her own way, offers the greatest gift one can give to another: belief in him or her.

The actualizer integrates his or her expression and guidance. The actualizer does not think *for* others but *with* others, having his or her own opinions and beliefs at the same time he or she allows others to have theirs.

II. The Goals of Actualization

CHAPTER 7

Honestly Being Your Feelings

"Don't be upset! Control yourself. Take it easy," cautions the manipulator. And well that person might, for dealing with feelings is a big part of his or her problem. Manipulators always prevent you from confronting them with the impact of your ideas or emotions. They cannot allow you to get angry with them anymore than they can allow you to get close to them.

A major defense against manipulation, our own and others, would be for us to learn how to become honestly expressive of our feelings.

THE NATURE OF FEELINGS

The truth is that most of us do not understand what it means to experience our feelings either physiologically or consciously, even though we live with them every day of our lives. As a result, we have never learned to communicate our feelings directly, effectively, or accurately. We spend a lot of our time telling others what we *think* rather than what we *feel*. Often our body language and tone of voice belie what we say, and we wonder why others don't seem to get our messages. Confusion prevails because we have sentenced ourselves to lives in a "tower of Babel." Many of us do not realize that we really feel our emotions in our bodies. It would be useful, therefore, to look at the five basic emotions and their physical manifestations.

1. *Anger*. What is the physiological evidence when you feel angry? How do you know when you are angry? You feel as if you want to fight. Your body stiffens; you breathe faster; your heart beats rapidly; you get tense and have the sensation of heat. When you are angry, a great deal of physical energy builds up, and your body feels as if it must do something. Expressing anger by saying things like "I'm so angry right now I feel like sending you to the moon without a space ship," is good medicine. Repressed anger is dangerous to your body and your relationships.

2. *Fear*. How do you know when your body is fearful? The feeling is almost the opposite of anger. Your mouth gets dry; you feel cold; your palms begin to sweat. Shake hands with someone who is frightened, and you usually will feel the cold sweat.

3. *Hurt*. Most of us seem afraid to admit hurt even to ourselves. It feels weakening to be hurt. It feels like a swift blow to the chest. Emotional hurt is painful, and we sure want to avoid pain. When we really feel hurt, we often act angry to cover it up. Or we simply push it deep inside. Back in childhood, no doubt, someone told us that big kids don't cry. In *Courage to Be*, Tillich says that most of us don't have the "courage of despair"—we are actually afraid to feel bad. Yet, unexpressed hurt can be a noose about the

neck of an individual that stifles all feeling. We recall all too poignantly the desperate look in the eyes of a man who blurted: "I wish more than anything that I could have a real 24-carat feeling of being hurt." Habits of a lifetime denied him the enormous relief of melting into tears.

4. *Joy.* If you have ever watched the fans when the underdog team has just scored the winning touchdown, you have an idea of the physical manifestation of joy. One's whole body tingles in delight. The body surges with energy. It is impossible to be tired or depressed when joy surfaces. Football games, or any sport, are where we give ourselves permission, en masse, to express the joy we ordinarily withhold in our attempts to maintain "dignity." Somewhere in our lives we learned to keep our delight hidden away. Perhaps we got the superstitious notion that if the gods knew of our joy, they would take it away. Or if others noticed us acting happy, they would try to rob us of our delight. Or if our internal topdog got too boisterous, our underdog would bring us to defeat. Joylessness is a malady of adulthood. Wordsworth says it well in "Ode: Intimations of Immortality":

> Shades of the prison-house begin to close
>   Upon the growing Boy,
> But he beholds the light, and whence it flows,
>   He sees it in his joy . . .
> At length the Man perceives it die away,
> And fade into the light of common day.

For some of us, it is possible to recall the feelings of joy we experienced in early childhood before we allowed adult worries and responsibilities to dim the light of our perceptions. As grown-ups, we became poor receivers of those things that ignite joy. There is a great truth in Christ's statement that we must be "like little children to enter into the kingdom of Heaven." Joylessness is like a banquet we refuse to taste, a magnificent sunset we refuse to see, a lovely concerto we refuse to hear, or a loving touch we refuse to feel. It is like being in heaven, but thinking only of hell. If joy is an emotion we cannot create at will, it is one we don't want to willfully deny ourselves when it arises.

5. Finally there is *love*. Love is many things, but it is also a feeling. Physiologically, love feels like a welling-up in the center of our bodies, accompanied by a desire to touch and hold the loved one. Rainer Maria Rilke, the German poet, said in *Letters to a Young Poet:* Love consists in this, that two solitudes protect and touch and greet each other." Love in all of its manifestations is the primary way we are able to step across the boundaries of our solitude to make contact with others.

Love's authenticity is commensurate with the lover's ability to experience and express anger, fear, hurt, and joy. To express love to another, we have to be able to express the four other feelings, and certainly this has important implications in human relationships, especially marriage. For example, one person can never have a true and lasting relationship with another until he or she is able to fight with the other. Love and anger are complementary opposites. Often we find that our warmest feelings of love rise out of the heat of anger. Honestly expressing anger resolves conflicts more quickly and reduces resentment on both sides. When we are able to show that we are angry, that we are afraid, that we can be hurt, that we can be joyful—then we can love. When we really level with each other and tell the other how we feel, only then do we begin to feel closeness. Love, by this set of standards, is clearly the true fulfillment of all other feelings.

MANIPULATING THE FEELINGS OF OTHERS

When all five feelings are expressed honestly, the individual is more real, more actualized. But manipulators, aware of the power of feelings, will try to use them to control others.

1. *Anger.* By using anger, a manipulator attempts to intimidate and create fear in others. All of us have met manipulators who by their shouting and screaming keep others from communicating with them. Some manipulators provoke anger in others in order to play the role of the weak victim of the brutal attack. The weak victim can then easily shame the other into compliance. "Gotcha!"

2. *Fear.* Eugene Burdick suggests that a manipulator uses fear in tandem with hate. "He sits at the console and gives 'em what he thinks they need; a little fear today, a little hate tomorrow. Some days he gives them both. And they stand together and shiver and think he's the greatest guy in the world and [they] love him."[1]

3. *Hurt.* The "silent treatment" is a tried and true favorite of manipulators. The manipulator looks as if he or she has been auditioning for a sinus medication commercial. Note the squint of the eyes, the furrow of the brow, the downward curve of the lips—the pained expression that can only come from eight undrained sinus cavities. But no matter how many entreaties the victim makes to find out what is wrong, the response is

always, "I'm okay. What makes you think something is wrong? Don't mind me, I'll just go to bed early."

4. *Joy.* Manipulators don't like to express joy they might feel, and they sure don't want anyone else to either. They are the joy killers: "You're sure lucky you got an A on your term paper, but I've heard that Professor Green grades easy on papers and hard on the final exam."

5. *Love,* perhaps the least likely to be thought of as a manipulative weapon, is paradoxically one of the most common manipulative techniques. How often has the phrase "If you loved me, you would . . ." been used to win a point, gain a goal, or exert control over a partner? A clever manipulator can use love to dominate a relationship or, conversely, to bring one to an end by saying, for example, "If you really loved me, you'd let me go."

COUNTERFEIT EMOTIONS

Before we can achieve the creative awareness we need to overcome the manipulations in our lives, we must learn to identify, experience, and honestly express real feelings, not counterfeit emotions. Some of the manipulator's repertoire of counterfeit emotions follow.

1. *Substituting one emotion for another.* Many of us express anger when it's really hurt we feel. We feel less vulnerable when we pretend anger instead of express hurt. Thus we hear the lady, tears welling in her eyes, cry out: "You make me so mad!" She isn't mad at all; she's hurt. Her body doesn't lie.

Using the same counterfeit pattern, we express anger when we are really afraid. "You make me so angry when you forget to take your medicine," a young woman screams at her ill mother. Her anger hides her fear. She is worried about her mother's health and is afraid her mother might die if she does not take her medicine.

2. *Feelings as a delayed reaction.* Here we meet the person whose pace is so slow that he says: "I was mad at you last week." Last week? It took him a week to find out? Not really. He knew how he felt last week, but he was afraid to express it then for fear he would be attacked in return. A favorite ploy of the withdrawing and avoiding manipulator is to hide his or her real emotion at the time it is felt to avoid contact with another. The delayed reaction also provides an advantage to the manipulator: time to prepare a surprise attack. It is just another way to control rather than to make contact with another.

3. *Making a virtue of not having normal feelings, or pretending you don't.* Most of us know some couple who boast that they have never had a fight. Our response would have to be "Tommyrot!" Normal people who have any contact at all with each other must rub each other the wrong way at times. Of course, they have fights. They have them because they have normal feelings, as much as they would like to appear virtuously free of them.

4. *Confusing your feelings with facts.* You say to someone, "You're stupid!" Your statement isn't a fact at all, since you have not actually measured that person's intelligence. If you said instead, "I *feel* that you are stupid," then you would be stating a fact about your feelings, not a fact about the other individual's intelligence.

5. *Expressing your feelings as you are poised for*

flight. Such a person may let true feelings slip out, but is ready to run the instant anyone reacts to them. A sign of immaturity, such timidity stunts one's emotional growth and the development of relationships.

CONGRUENCE AND ACTUALIZATION

Congruence, as Carl Rogers defines it, is accurately matching experience with awareness.[2] It means to feel our feelings physically, to communicate them accurately, and to experience them consciously. If we can do all three, there is congruence.

The manipulator is not congruent. When our heads are out of sync with our heart, we are said to be *deceitful.* For example, when we tell the hostess we had a good time at her party when actually we were bored, we are not expressing what we feel internally. Being perfectly honest, but still polite, we might say, "Thank you for inviting us."

When the manipulator's conscious awareness is out of phase with his or her physiological awareness, the person is said to be *defensive.* For example, a man may express anger behaviorally, while denying it verbally. "Are you angry?" his friend asks. Clenching his fist and slamming it onto the table, he shouts, "No! I am not angry!" His body is angry, as anyone can plainly see, but he, unaware of his anger, cannot admit it. Rarely are the manipulator's words congruent with his body. Learning to pay attention to bodily sensations helps the manipulator to bring about a congruence between bodily and conscious awareness.

COMMUNICATING FEELINGS—
MANIPULATIVE PATTERNS

Two elements are involved in the communication of feelings: sending and receiving. Much like radio transmitters, we constantly send out messages. The question is whether we are reaching anyone. We all have some degree of difficulty in communicating accurately, in being understood. Manipulators have special problems in this area of communicating their feelings.

The first involves errors in sending, and one of these errors is the *unexpressed expectation.* It's Father's Day, let's say, and Dad has secretly hoped that his children will remember him with a small gift, a card, or a phone call. He hopes one of these things will happen, but he doesn't say anything about his expectation. When nothing happens—no gift, no card, no call—he is understandably disappointed. But the fault is largely his own. He made a sending error and allowed his expectations to go unvoiced.

Most personal relationships are based on such expectations. Yet, many of us seldom take the time or trouble—or we are afraid, really—to ask for the things we want.

The actualizer knows this, for he or she knows quite a bit about communication. The actualizer doesn't want to go through life being misunderstood. Knowing that many misunderstandings can be avoided by simple statements of need and want, the actualizer is able to ask for whatever he or she may want, no matter what it may be.

A second type of sending error is what we call the *contrived expectation.* This can be described as manipulating another's response by the way we state our expectation. We exaggerate our expectation. One overweight little boy, intent on eating a juicy red apple, begs his mother for some cookies. She offers the apple as an alternative, which is what he wanted all along. Or the wife who complains to her husband, "You didn't get home until two A.M.," knowing it was probably much earlier, in order to get him to admit that he got home at one in the morning.

The other communication problem is in receiving, where we make just as many errors. For instance, we may appear to ignore a message that we really aren't ignoring at all. Someone says something that hurts us quite badly, but we won't say, "That hurts." We ignore it; we simply don't respond at all as we continue to nurse our hurt.

Another receiving error occurs when we *neutralize the communication* sent to us. This may very well be a measure of our ability to receive love. Someone says: "You look lovely tonight." We do not reply, "Thank you, I appreciate the compliment." Rather, we respond: "Oh, you look lovely, too." It's almost as if we are afraid to feel good when someone gives us warm and caring messages. We keep throwing it back so we don't have to feel the impact of the good feeling. It is our underdog, insisting we are not worthy, that cancels out the gifts of love.

A third receiving error is always *responding in terms of the expectations of others*. No matter what they say, we give back what we think they want to hear, denying our own feelings. "Do you like my new suit?" coaxes a friend. You reply dutifully, "Oh, I think it looks great." The truth of your feelings may be that you wonder how your friend could have bought such a turkey. You might reply more honestly, "Well, I like the cut of the jacket," or even, "No, I can't say I do." There is nothing wrong with disagreeing, especially in matters of taste.

Finally, we may *respond as if the other person's message is contrived!* "What is it she really wants to know?" you might wonder. "I have to figure out what she really wants so I won't give it to her." A husband who had entertained clients (which included an ex-girlfriend) for lunch, is asked by his wife, "How was your lunch meeting today?" He assumes her question is contrived, for obvious reasons, and he's just not going to give her the reply she wants. So he answers, "The same old thing."

ACTUALIZING COMMUNICATION PATTERNS

Actualization involves honestly being your feelings in both receiving communications and in sending them. It involves some risks, or at least perceived risks, to those of us who habitually distrust our feelings and how others will react to them. The rewards of honest communication of feelings are immense. Others will sense your realness, your integrity and honesty, and will be more willing to reciprocate in kind. The frequency of misunderstanding each other will be less. The amount of mental and emotional energy you expend in relationships with others will also be lightened. That drained, tired feeling that comes from manipulation will dissipate.

A solid principle of actualization is that a healthy

relationship does not always have to be an agreeing relationship. Some of our most productive family, social, and work relationships exist because we accept the fact that different people have different points of view and feelings about things, and that we respect those differences. Often in life we make the erroneous assumption that in order to have harmony we must also have agreement. An actualizer is an appreciater of differences.

An actualizer who honestly feels is particularly aware of the danger of pretense. The actualizer doesn't pretend to care when he or she doesn't, or pretends not to care when he or she does. The actualizer avoids such stock phrases as "I give up," "You win," and "I've had it." Instead, the actualizer honestly expresses dislikes, wants, and hopes, believing that directness is the means whereby love is maintained and strengthened.

Honestly recognizing and living with your feelings cracks the wall that manipulation has built between you and others.

NOTES

1. Eugene Burdick, *The Ninth Wave* (Boston: Houghton Mifflin Company, 1956). p. 90.
2. Carl Rogers, *On Becoming a Person* (Boston: Houghton Mifflin Company, 1961), p. 282.

CHAPTER 8

Contact vs. Manipulation

An actualizing relationship between two people takes place when one person relates to another core-to-core. By "core," we mean the one's inner range of potentials. This inner core may also be called one's real self.

Through expressing a variety of passive and active potentials, such as caring and assertiveness, actualizers open paths for the spontaneous "understanding" of themselves and others. Very good friends, as we know, are said to communicate sensitivity to each other. This is contact. A wife may communicate with her husband with as little as a smile or a sigh if their relationship is core-to-core. To understand the difference between contact and manipulation, see Figure 5.

Contact is shown as the touching of two inner cores of actualizing potentials, which we call core-to-core contact. In contrast, manipulation is shown as distant interaction between the outer rings, the surface of each personality. This we call role-to-role manipula-

Figure 5

Contact vs. Manipulation

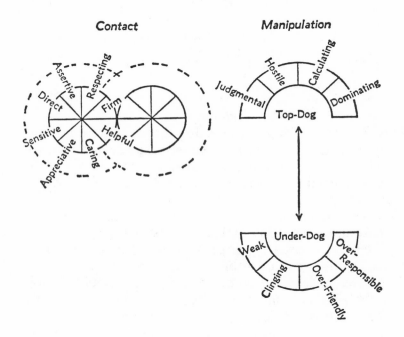

tion. The manipulative relationship is not intimate, but distant.

As you can see, contact is a form of loving or trusting another person in a relationship of closeness. Manipulation is a relationship of distance, a withdrawal to less personal or intense forms of communication. Core-to-core contact is based on the truth of each self, whereas role-to-role manipulation is based to some extent on deceit and mistrust.

Daniel Defoe's novel *Moll Flanders* provides an extreme example of role-to-role manipulation. It seems that Moll, the impoverished heroine of the novel, wishes to make contact with a man of wealth, any man of wealth, for the purpose of matrimony. To attract such a man, she plays, of course, the role of a wealthy young woman. It seems that a young man, currently out of funds, wishes to make contact with a woman of wealth, also for the purpose of matrimony. He plays the role of a wealthy young man. You guessed it. They find each other and marry, each certain the other can pay the debts they incurred in creating their wealthy roles. Each is justifiably disillusioned.

Core-to-core contact is not a permanent state. Indeed, it is a fragile thing to be developed at each meeting between two individuals. It develops when at least one of the persons is able to be freely expressive rather than calculatedly impressive—honestly expressive of self rather than deceitful. It is also facilitated when at least one of the parties is willing to really listen to the other person and to respond to the other person's statements and feelings accurately. In a way, being real is catching. If you are able to present yourself wholly, with both your strengths and weaknesses, with both your assertiveness and lovability, you will in time be able to break down the guardedness, defensiveness, and deceit of the other person. You will have begun to create the fertile ground for a truly core-to-core relationship.

But a core-to-core relationship is not easy to sustain. Manipulators fear vulnerability, fear being exposed or judged. They are afraid that sustained contact with another will reveal a dimension of themselves that they have so far denied or refused to see.

True personal contact involves emotional risk. But the manipulator chooses to avoid risk by attempting to control those around him or her. Consider the case of a father and his fourteen-year-old daughter, discussing whether or not she can go on a chaperoned, co-ed weekend camping trip.

"No way will I allow you to go!" says the father. "I won't permit it!"

"But, Dad, I've been looking forward to it for weeks," his daughter says.

"Absolutely not!" repeats the father, exerting dominance. He avoids saying what is really on his mind: his concern that the girl will experiment with sex during the weekend. In his zeal to be a good, competent father, which he secretly fears he is not, he resorts to controlling rather than contacting. His wife, having overhead the argument and intuitively sensing his unspoken concern, later tells him, "You needn't worry that she'll get into trouble. If you would let yourself be closer to her, you'd know that; you'd know the kind of young woman she is."

At this point, the conversation might open up a vital and valuable discussion between the parents, for this father truly wants to be closer to his daughter. The

The Goals of Actualization

trouble is that he is afraid of expressing that sense of caring. There can be many reasons for his fear. Perhaps—to cite one possibility—he was so controlled as a child by his mother that he draws away from the risk of closeness with any woman, or with women in general. All the man can do, then, is turn the charge back upon his wife, shouting: "You're the one who's not close to her!"

Rather than get into a core-to-core conversation about his feelings, which might reveal his fear of caring for his daughter, the father changes the topic. To avoid a discussion of feelings, he diverts the conversation to a safely "intellectual" topic: "Her school grades aren't that great, you know. She could use this weekend to stay home and study." Instead of trying to see the situation from the girl's point of view, the man denies his core-caring as he might express it were he able to be in contact with her.

Consider the bank loan officer. She felt so insecure about her competence that she hid behind a persona of officiousness and super-efficiency. No one could get close to her. Customers, no matter how desperate for a loan, would delay applying if they thought they would have to deal with her and her cold, controlled manner. One day, however, she felt so overwhelmed with paperwork and so isolated that she actually uttered the unspeakable to a customer: "I can't seem to get on top of anything today. I'll probably be here until midnight, trying to catch up." To her surprise, the customer smiled at her and said, "Gee. I know what you mean. I've been feeling that way, too. Only it's going to take *me* about a year!" The barrier dropped, and the two women were able to chat amiably. Risking being her self brought the loan officer an unexpected response. Instead of being judged, as she had feared, she was understood. And her customer felt understood as well. A short, but real, core-to-core contact was made.

Manipulators have to control everything—themselves, others, even conversations. They choose the topics. They evaluate rather than appreciate. They try to convince others, rather than exchange ideas with others. Or they limit themselves to safe "small talk." In many people, generalities such as the weather might be a prelude to contact, but in manipulators, more often than not, they are only a means of avoiding personal contact.

Jay Haley suggests several ways the manipulator seeks to control communication.

• *By denying that he is communicating.* "I think you should apologize to him, but it's not my place to tell you." (He has said it but at the same time denies that he has.)

• *By denying the message itself.* "Oh, forget it; I guess it wasn't important." Or she insists the message is misunderstood: "You didn't get the point."

• *By denying that the message is communicated to the other person.* "I was just talking to myself . . . just thinking out loud. . . ."

• *By denying the context or situation.* "You always make fun of me" (referring to the past). "You will think I'm silly" (referring to the future). In both examples he avoids dealing with the person *now.*[1]

CORE RELATIONSHIPS VS. SUPERFICIAL RELATIONSHIPS

A core relationship is contact between two individuals who express and reveal themselves to each other openly and honestly, appreciating and accepting each other as they truly are and trusting in the abilities and goodwill of each other. A core relationship can be longstanding—a husband and wife, a parent and child, close friends, business partners—or it can be briefer and more casual—a clerk at the supermarket and a customer, co-workers, parents of children who play together. Any possible encounter between two people can have the characteristics of a core relationship.

Have you ever met someone, had a conversation, then moved on, probably never to see that person again, but you felt really good about yourself and about that person? Felt that you had received something wonderful and had given something wonderful? If so, you have had a core-to-core relationship, however brief, with another individual. One or both of you revealed yourselves honestly and openly, appreciated and accepted each other as you truly are, and trusted each other's abilities and goodwill.

By comparison, superficial relationships can be found as readily in longstanding contacts—such as with husbands and wives, parents and children—as in more casual interactions. The characteristics of superficial relationships are unawareness, control, deception, distrust, criticism, and petty competitiveness. Manipulators take a lot of time and expend a great deal of energy on superficial relationships. They cultivate them, make them happen. And when they go home at night, they are too tired even to be civil to those they should be closest to, their families.

We believe that core-to-core relationships do not always take time and energy, but that they do take the willingness to be aware, honest, trusting, accepting, and appreciative. The enhancement of self and others in such relationships is beyond measure.

EMOTIONS: CONTACT VS. CONTROL

Emotions are the primary means by which we make contact. Emotions need to be expressed to be complete. Take the feeling of excitement. It seeks to express itself in contact with other human beings. Excitement, the basic life energy of the individual, is almost inconceivable without a recipient of that force. A child who gets an "A" on her spelling test bursts with excitement until she can get home to tell her mother. Or the young man who has just seen a wonderful movie can't wait to tell his best friend about it.

The five basic emotions of anger, fear, hurt, joy, and love are also incomplete if we do not express them, share them with another. Likewise, core relationships cannot grow, or even exist for that matter, if we cannot express our emotional life. It is no wonder the manipulator fails to form such relationships and suffers the maladies of blocked emotions.

The manipulator, blocking anger, might be said to be seething with resentment. This anger is incomplete and eventually, turned inward, results in feelings of resignation and depression.

Fear keeps the manipulator imprisoned when she or he does not express it. The manipulator becomes a worrier, nibbling at the edges of the prison cell, unable to break free of phobias.

Hurt, when not expressed, cannot be finished with. It, too, simmers inside to become a pervasive, long-lasting sadness that threatens normal self-esteem.

Repressed joy can destroy ambition, intellectual development, inquisitiveness, and awareness. Joy is the pay-off for almost everything we do, and without it life and its challenges become nothing more than drudgery.

Unrequited love may be sad, but unexpressed love is a tragedy. It provides the manipulator with a lifetime of regret over what might have been. Withholding caring, or incomplete love, is like giving a stone to another instead of bread. It affects adversely both the one who would not give and the one who does not, therefore, receive.

CONTACT AND WITHDRAWAL

Meaningful contact with others requires an ability to be quite comfortable with yourself alone. Manipulators who are withdrawing and avoiding might appear to like to be alone. This is not true. Such manipulators are equally as *un*comfortable with themselves as they are with others. Actualizers, on the other hand, enjoying close contact with others, also cherish their moments of privacy. One of the subjects of Maslow's study of self-actualizing people sat alone for one hour a day, between five and six in the evening, in front of her fireplace. That time was sacred to her, and other concerns were not allowed to interfere.

If you examine your daily routine, you will find that you are "withdrawn" for approximately eight hours during sleep. You are more or less involved with other people at work for another eight hours, which leaves about eight hours for relationships with family and friends. About half of our existence, then, involves people. It would be unnatural to want a great deal more. No matter how self-actualizing you may be, you must at times be by yourself.

Although manipulation usually involves withdrawal from close relationships, one can be manipulative by maintaining a relationship beyond its nourishing value. Such a manipulator is described by Perls as a clinger or hanging-on biter.[2] The clingers won't give up, but keep right on talking to you although they realize that the conversation is finished. This is not a matter of social awkwardness, of not knowing how to terminate the exchange, but a neurotic fear on the part of these individuals that they haven't said all they want to say. They are so insecure that they can't let go. This fear costs people jobs when they go for interviews and, having said something once, they keep trying to say it again and invariably mess it all up. The hanging-on biters are those recognizable individuals who hang on to a conversation like a bulldog with a stick. Rather than bite it off, they brace themselves like a bulldog and stand there, vigorously shaking the conversational stick.

NOTES

1. Jay Haley, *Strategies of Psychotherapy* (New York: Grune & Stratton, 1963), pp. 89-90.
2. Frederick Perls, *Ego, Hunger and Aggression* (London: George Allen and Unwin, 1947), p. 108.

CHAPTER 9

Trusting Yourself in the Here and Now

One of the significant differences between the manipulator and the actualizer lies in the way each approaches the dimension of time. Past, present, and future exist for both of them, of course. But each uses these three aspects of the flow of time in vastly different ways.

For the manipulator, past events—real or imagined—conveniently provide excuses for failures. The future (since in one sense it never really arrives) is where manipulators can base their promises. As for the present-oriented manipulators, they talk a lot about what they are doing and may seem to be busy, but in fact they seldom accomplish much of anything.

PRESENT VS. PAST AND FUTURE

From our studies[1] of the time-orientation of manipulators, we have come to the following conclusions:

1. The past-oriented manipulator is characterized

by guilt, regret, remorse, blaming and resentments. He or she never lets go of past hurts, never wipes the slate clean of unhappy memories. Listen to the manipulator, and you will hear such things as:

- I feel so bad about what happened to my dad. Life has no meaning for me now.

- If only my parents had encouraged me to stay in college, I'd have my degree now. It's too late to go back, and it's all their fault.

- Our marriage would have lasted if only my wife had stopped nagging, or if only my husband had paid more attention to me.

- My boss is completely unreasonable! How does he expect me to do a good job for him?

2. The future-oriented manipulators continually live in a world that does not yet exist. Their days are filled with idealized goals, high expectations, elaborate plans, grandiose predictions—and nagging fears. They are obsessive worriers who project their hopes and anxieties into the future.

- Someday I'll get going and return to school. I've got too many responsibilities now.

- You wait and see, I'll be working here long after those guys are gone.

- I'm so worried about what is going to happen, I just can't do anything right.

- I promise to do better next time.

90

3. Manipulators who are present-oriented are individuals whose past does not contribute to the present in any meaningful way and who have no future goals tied to present activity. They keep feverishly busy, but all their activity is a way to avoid facing themselves. They would say:

- I've got so many responsibilities right now, I just don't have time to think.

- I have three children and a spouse to care for, and I don't have time for myself.

- I've made a list of all the things I'm doing today.

Actualizing persons, on the other hand, are primarily time-competent. They are concerned with living fully in the present, but use the past and future to make the present more meaningful. They understand that memory and anticipation are *acts in the present.* The focus, therefore, of the actualizing individual is on the present with the past and future as background.

Past, present, and future are, to the actualizing individual, a *gestalt*—a whole. Figure 6 is a textbook, visual example of the "figure-ground" phenomenon. The gray areas, if seen as background, define the figure of the white chalice in the center. Likewise, the white area, if seen as background, defines the figure of the two heads in profile. In a sense, then, the figure of the chalice (the present) is defined by the gray background (past and future); and the figures of the two profiles (past and future) are defined by the figure of the chalice (the present).

Figure 6

Time as "Figure/Ground"

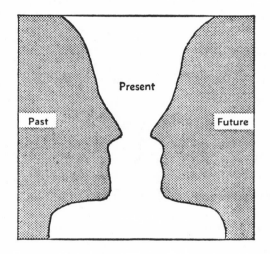

Present

Past

Future

It is impossible to see both figures at the same time. One must choose. The actualizer accepts the unchangeable particulars of the past and the indefiniteness of the future, and focuses on the part over which he or she has most power: the reality of the present.

PRESENT ORIENTATION
AND ACTUALIZATION

Our research shows a parallel or correlation between actualization and time competence.[2] Self-actualizing people, those who trust in self-support, are oriented to the here and now.

"I have tried to express this," said Maslow, "as a contrast between *living fully* and *preparing* to live fully, between *growing up* and *being grown.*"[3] Actualizers are functioning *now*. Manipulators are paralyzed by regret (the past) and intent (the future). Manipulators talk a lot.

"Things were better then." (the good old days).
"He ruined my life twenty years ago when he . . ."
(the bad old days).
"Everything will be okay someday, if only. . . ."
(supernatural intervention).
"I don't know what I'll do if . . ." (dire prediction).

But they function only marginally.

Persons who live in the future rely on expected events to motivate them. Frederick Perls suggests that ideals or goals are means by which the manipulator's need for affection, appreciation, and admiration is gratified. That is, manipulators gratify their vanity by picturing themselves in terms of their goals. They invent a meaning for life to justify their experience. But by this very striving for the goal of future perfections, manipulators turn their lives into a living hell. They achieve just the opposite of their intentions, arresting their own development and promoting feelings of inferiority in themselves. By the same token, individuals who live in the past rely on blaming others as a substitute for self-support.

Our problems exist in the here and now, regardless of when they were born, and their solutions must be found in the here and now. Quite literally, the only time we *can* live is in the present. We can remember the past; we can anticipate the future, but we live only in the present. Even when we reexperience the past, we have not reversed time. We have, in effect, only moved the past up to the present. So if psychotherapy is to help us solve our problems, it must work within the framework we have: the here and now.

It is important to stress again that memory (from the past) and anticipation (toward the future) are acts in the present. "Now here I am *remembering* my mistakes," says the patient. Note the difference between that and merely wandering off into memory. Or one might say: "I am *planning* to do the job on Wednesday," and we would have to consider it as more than idle anticipation.

Manipulators who are given to reminiscence of the past or idle talk of the future are not refreshed by these mental wanderings. They are exhausted and emptied, for such behavior is not active but passive. As Perls implies, one's worthiness cannot be put forth in explanations for the past or by promises for the future.

"It wasn't my fault," whines the manipulator in referring to the past. "I'm as good as anybody else." Referring to the future, he says: "I'm not very well right now, but I'll make my mark."

Unlike either of these, actualizers get their feelings of worthiness from their adequacy in an activity that is going on now, or in relaxation after finishing it. They feel that explaining or promising is a lie, either a consoling or a self—punishing one. But to *do* something and to *be* oneself are self-trusting and self-justifying. Here are examples of self-actualizing, *present* behavior.

- I feel so alive working in the yard today.
- I really got a lot done today.

Looking more closely at the concept of the healthy individual as one who lives primarily in the present, we see that living fully in the moment requires no concern for external support or sustenance. To say, "I *am* adequate now" rather than "I *was* adequate once" or "I *will be* adequate again" is self-validating and self-justifying. Just being in the moment is sufficient and is an end in itself. *Being has its own reward— a feeling of trust in one's self-support.* Experiencing self-support, a by-product of living in the present, is being "inner-directed" as opposed to "other-directed."[4]

Maslow said that a person experiencing time in this way is one living in a state of "creative innocence."

In the child there is a total unquestioning acceptance of whatever happens. Since there is also very little memory, *very little leaning on the past*, there is

95

little tendency in the child to bring the past into the present or into the future. The consequence is that the child is totally without past or future.

If one expects nothing, if one has no anticipations or apprehensions, if in a certain sense *there is no future,* because the child is moving totally "here—now," there can be no surprise, no disappointment. One thing is as likely as another to happen. This is "perfect waiting" and spectatorship without any demands that one thing happen rather than another. There is no prognosis. And no prediction means no worry, no anxiety, no apprehension or foreboding.

This is all related to my conception of the creative personality as one who is totally here—now, *one who lives without future or past.* Another way of saying this is: "The creative person is an innocent." An innocent could be defined as a grown person who can still perceive, or think or react like a child. It is this innocence that is recovered in the "second naivete, or perhaps I will call it the "second innocence" of the wise old man who has managed to recover the ability to be childlike.[5]

The manipulators may be past-oriented and using the past as an excuse for failure. They may be future-oriented and using the future for promises that never materialize. Or they may be present-oriented and using the present to talk about everything they are doing but getting none of it done. In any event, they spend most of their time justifying and defending themselves: If they are underdog manipulators, they are criers or blamers, asking for love in spite of bad luck. If they are topdog manipulators, they con us into psuedo-support and justification, in that the deception of another person gives them a feeling of power. If they were deeply honest, they would have to admit that their ventures are empty and unfulfilling.

Actualizers, on the other hand (as always), are doers, be-ers. They express feelings and talents in an effort to cope with life in the present. They feel good about themselves because their existence is filled with ongoing activity. They experience self-support and self-expression in living life in the here and now. They move freely into the past for memories and into the future for goals, but remember that these, too, are acts of the present from which self-support comes.

For actualizers, life is an exciting process of trusting themselves in the here and now.

NOTES

1. Everett L. Shostrom, *Personal Orientation Inventory* (San Diego: Educational and Industrial Testing Service, 1964).
2. "A Test for the Measurement of Self-Actualization," *Educational and Psychological Measurement*, XXIV (1965): 207-18.
3. Abraham H. Maslow, *Toward a Psychology of Being* (Princeton, N.J.: D. Van Nostrand & Co., 1962), p. 30.
4. These terms have been adapted from David Riesman, *The Lonely Crowd* (Garden City, N.Y.: Doubleday Anchor Books, 1950).
5. Abraham H. Maslow, "Innocent Cognition (as an aspect of B-Cognition)," *Notes on B-Psychology* (La Jolla, Calif.: Western Behavioral Sciences Institute, August 31, 1961): 1-2.

CHAPTER 10

Freedom and Awareness

"What is man that thou art mindful of him?" the psalmist asks. The question strikes to the heart of the human condition, for while the need to understand ourselves is all-important, the process of doing so is a complex one. One of the measures of the greatness of writers down through the ages is that they have given us some insights, some answers. In *Resurrection*, Leo Tolstoy includes this cogent paragraph:

> One of the most widespread superstitions is that every man has his own special, definite qualities; that a man is kind, cruel, wise, stupid, energetic, apathetic, etc. Men are not like that . . . men are like rivers: the water is the same in each, and alike in all; but every river is narrow here, is more rapid there, here slower, there broader, now clear, now cold, now dull, now warm. It is the same with men. Every man carries in himself the germs of every human quality, and sometimes one manifests itself, sometimes another, and the man often becomes unlike himself, while still remaining the same man.

We have suggested that persons can be separated into, or identified by, two broad categories of behavior: the manipulator and the actualizer. Yet, as Tolstoy tells us, each person has within herself or himself the potential of every human quality.

What that means, then, is that while each person is a manipulator, he or she is (or can be) also an actualizer. The important fact seems to be that each of us has a continuing choice, each of us is free to choose one or the other.

So far in this section, we have explored two of the qualities that we believe are prime requirements for actualization. One is the honest use of feelings and *honesty* of expression. The other is the deep *trust* an actualizer has in the self and in others, a trust that allows him or her to cope with life in the here and now. We come now to two other important qualities that characterize the actualizer: freedom and awareness.

By "freedom" we do not simply mean freedom from the control of others, but rather the freedom to actualize, to be our best, real selves. Freedom is the choice we make and the responsibility we take for a style of expression we use.[1] Erich Fromm believes that we have "the freedom to create, to construct, to wonder, to venture." He goes on to define freedom as the capacity to make a choice, to choose between alternatives.[2] Yet, only when we are aware of our manipulations are we free to experience them and to derive from them actualizing behavior.

Actualizers are free in the sense that, while they may play the game of life, they are aware that they are playing it. They play it "tongue in cheek," Alan Watts says. They realize that they sometimes manipulate and at other times are manipulated. But in both cases, *they are aware of the manipulation.* They do not try to change the manipulator, lest, at that moment, the actualizers become manipulators themselves. Taking the responsibility to change another is, paradoxically, to be manipulated by that person. One may describe the other person as a manipulator, or confront that person with his or her manipulation, but one need not take responsibility to change that person. The actualizer recognizes that each person must ultimately take that responsibility for himself or herself.

Actualizers also realize that life need not be a serious game, but rather more akin to a dance. No one wins or loses in a dance; a dance is a process. Actualizers dance among all their complementary potentials. What is important is to enjoy the process of living rather than to achieve the *ends* of living. Since actualizing people appreciate *doing* for its own sake, they enjoy the process of getting someplace as much as the arriving. The actualizer does not take life with dead seriousness. Manipulators, on the other hand, see life as a competition, a rat race, something to be conquered. They take life so seriously that they are frequently candidates for nervous breakdowns.

SURRENDER OR NONSTRIVING

Our Western culture rests generally on Judeo-Christian theology, and the United States is dominated particularly by a puritan spirit that stresses activity, striving, and hard work.[3] Karen Horney speaks of the Apollonian and Dionysian tendencies, the latter stressing the value of surrender and drift, the former emphasizing the mastery and molding of life. Both are natural human tendencies, she says, but the

100

positive value of surrender or nonstriving is a deep-rooted attitude, pregnant with potential satisfaction.[4]

Alan Watts puts the value of nonstriving in still another context:

> I have always been fascinated by the law of reversed effort. Sometimes I call it the "backwards law." When you try to stay on the surface of the water, you sink; but when you try to sink, you float. When you hold your breath you lose it—which immediately calls to mind an ancient and most neglected saying, "Whosoever would save his soul shall lose it." Insecurity is the result of trying to be secure, and that, contrariwise, salvation and sanity consist in the most radical recognition that we have no way of saving ourselves. The Chinese sage Lao-tzu, that master of the law of reversed effort . . . declared that those who justify themselves do not convince, that to know the truth one must get rid of knowledge, and that nothing is more powerful and creative than emptiness—from which men shrink.[5]

What Watts is saying is that the more we try in some situations, the more we seem to fail, and that there are some goals that can never be achieved by active striving. We find this particularly true in psychotherapy, when the more one tries to become a certain way, the more one fails.

Leslie H. Farber speaks of the paradoxical nature of certain qualities of being and the impossibility of striving for such qualities as wisdom, dignity, courage, and humility. The element that characterizes each of these virtues is that one's possession of them lies outside of conscious effort. As Farber observes:

> Most accomplishments and some virtues do not have this *paradoxical* nature. Skill or tact or a capacity for honesty, for example, may be pursued directly; to acknowledge and enjoy possession of them does not contradict their nature. But only the fool proclaims his wisdom, only the proud man his humility, only the coward his courage. Not only do these virtues make a liar of the man who claims them, they forever evade any effort to achieve them. I may seek knowledge; I may not seek to be wise. Sharing an essential freedom from self-concern . . . such virtues are not accomplishments and cannot be learned. They must be deserved, but their possession is a matter of grace.[6]

Understanding this concept is extremely important as a basis of self-actualization, for it means that the most profound qualities of actualization—such as wisdom, dignity, humility, courage, respect, and love—*cannot be striven for!* They cannot be learned. And they are most often achieved when one surrenders to the impossibility of being wise, dignified, humble, courageous, respectful, and loving.

In psychotherapy, for example, we hear a patient striving to be "real"; the more she strives, the phonier she becomes. After many hours, she finally says, "I give up. I just can't seem to make it." In that moment, paradoxically, she is real! The religious provides another example: The more he strives to be humble, the more he becomes proud. Curiously, the most lovable person is one who has truly given up trying to be lovable!

This is why therapy for actualization and realness requires something more than motivated striving and simple conditioning. It requires being able to discover the wealth of personal growth instead of striving for it. Four characteristics of actualization—honesty, trust, freedom, and awareness—share this paradoxical quality. They can be accomplished by engaging in a process, but the process requires that the patient give up striving to be honest, trusting, free, and aware.

OMNIPOTENCE OR HUMANNESS?

Manipulators never have learned the secret of balance between authentic surrender and honest striving. They are instead junior gods who try to run their lives and the lives of others by control and manipulation. They have a deeply rooted attitude of distrust in themselves and others. Even their passive, helpless manipulations are a form of striving for omnipotence, in that the helpless one always controls and directs the active ones in his or her life. The active demanding and "shoulding" of a manipulator are also forms of omnipotence that display a deep distrust of other persons' potential for independent action.

Actualization is the alternative that offers humanness. It offers belief in oneself and in one's full potentials, valuing one's limitations, and loving oneself in spite of these limitations. Actualizers balance their polarities of love and anger, weakness and strength, allowing each full measure in their day-to-day experience. Actualizers believe that their organisms, as made, can be trusted to work in their efforts to cope with the problems of living.

AWARENESS

Possibly the most important idea we can offer is that the human need not be a manipulator and, equally important, need not be a helpless victim of manipulation.

With awareness, manipulation decreases and actualization increases.

A basic concept in Gestalt therapy is of the "continuum of awareness." This means that one can learn to focus on the ever-changing moment and express what she or he is experiencing from moment to moment. What we focus on at the moment seems to be summarized in three dimensions: (1) Here vs. There (someplace else), (2) Now vs. Past or Future, and (3) Feeling vs. Thinking.

The therapist, in helping a patient learn how to sharpen her awareness, continually asks her to finish this statement: "Here and now, I am aware that _____." The patient then describes what she is feeling, thinking, and sensing in the here and now. Her thinking consists either of remembering the past or planning the future. Her sensing is what she is now seeing or hearing. Her feeling is the emotions she is experiencing at the time. Consider the following conversation.

Therapist: Finish the statement, "Here and now I am aware that _____."

Patient: *Here and now I am aware that I am afraid.*

Therapist: Can you describe where you are feeling your fear?

104

Patient: *My voice is weak, and my hands are clammy.*

Therapist: What else are you aware of?

Patient: *I am aware of the air-conditioning noise in the room.*

Therapist: What else are you aware of?

Patient: *I'm aware of the rough texture of this chair arm.*

Therapist: Where are you feeling the roughness?

Patient: *I am aware of the roughness on the palm of my hand.*

Therapist: Are you aware that you are kicking your leg?

Patient: *I am aware that I am kicking my leg.*

Therapist: Who would you like to kick?

Patient: *You, for making me do these silly exercises!*

That interchange illustrates the importance of learning to be aware of the obvious. The manipulator customarily does not see or hear such small things as movements of hands and feet, facial expressions, posture and intonation in his or her voice or in the voices of others. But as he is guided to raise his awareness through exercises such as the above, he moves from deadness to aliveness. Instead of relying on calculated manipulations to deal with others, the manipulator is helped to trust his spontaneous reactions to his world.

Why is awareness so important? The reason is that *awareness is the first step to change.* Awareness really doesn't require striving. It requires looking and really seeing, listening and really hearing, touching and really feeling. It is impossible to manipulate someone if you are really listening to what that person is saying. Sometimes awareness even comes when you play your phony, manipulative role when seeking external support. Especially in the safety of a therapeutic setting, you can critically experience your manipulative roles—be your own "snotty, little self"—no matter how foolish or ridiculous they may be. The awareness comes when you both intellectually admit your phoniness and at the same time experience it emotionally. You can then experience the self-defeating quality of manipulation and become freer to create from these roles the complementary, actualizing behaviors. The following example, taken from a case history, will illustrate.

Therapist: What are you aware of now?
Patient: *I'm aware of wanting to hit you.*
Therapist: Be the you that wants to hit.
Patient: *I want to hit because you won't decide for me.*
Therapist: Now, be me and answer that.
Patient: *"You will never grow up if you keep getting me to make your decisions."*
Therapist: And what do you answer?
Patient: *You're right, darn you!*

By asking the patient to experience her dependent manipulation, and then by asking her to be the "wise therapist," the therapist gets her to discover and respect her own wise, actualizing potential, which lies deep within herself.

So we see that the road to emotional health runs through the expression of manipulative behaviors, not through rejection and striving for change! Awareness of the futility of manipulation leads to the power of self-actualization.

NOTES

1. Gene Sagar, unpublished manuscript.
2. Erich Fromm, *The Heart of Man*, ed. by Ruth N. Ashen (New York: Harper, 1964), pp. 52, 132.
3. Abraham H. Maslow, *Motivation and Personality* (New York: Harper, 1954), p. 291.
4. Karen Horney, *The Neurotic Personality of Our Time* (New York: W. W. Norton, 1937), pp. 270-75.
5. Alan W. Watts, *The Wisdom of Insecurity* (New York: Random House, 1949), pp. 9-10.
6. Leslie H. Farber, "Faces of Envy," *Review of Existential Psychology and Psychiatry*, I (Spring 1961): 134-35.

CHAPTER 11

Personal Control

In the next section of this book, we will show how the theories and principles we have been exploring in the last few chapters are applied in group therapy with real clients. Before we do that, however, we would like to suggest an ethic for the natural control of personal behavior, which can serve as a backdrop for the life situations we will be discussing.

As we've seen, human nature is characterized by polarities. Humans are active and passive, weak but strong, independent yet dependent, affectionate yet aggressive. They are both topdogs and underdogs. We would like to introduce two more general terms— *conservative* and *liberal*—chosen because of their universal usage and because of their non-moralistic connotations.

The two-party system of politics in America is a good example of the importance of giving credence to opposing viewpoints. In Great Britain, the party out of power is referred to as "Her Majesty's Loyal Opposition." In every one of us there is a similar two-party system, each with its loyal opposition, sometimes in power and sometimes not. We use the terms *liberal* and *conservative* to describe these several "me's" because they imply the truth, which is that both are parts of a potential unity. Too often people would repress or destroy one side or the other of this polarity. The truth is that ultimate mental health requires retaining, valuing, and living with both sides of ourselves.

The two sides of our psychological nature may be thought of as parallel to the two sides of our physical nature. We have right and left eyes, right and left ears, and so on. Recently a patient came in, complaining that her husband was unfaithful. She was afraid that he was about to leave her, and she wanted to save their marriage. As she talked, it became obvious that the left side of her body was paralyzed. She made every gesture with her right hand, while her left hand lay limply in her lap. She had been referred, she said, by her family physician, who could find no physical ailment to explain her handicap.

This woman, who for twenty years had been a kindergarten teacher, had been quite conventional and very conservative. It became quite clear that her entire orientation was "right." She always did the "right thing," said the "right thing," and never expressed a "different" point of view. In effect, she was dull and lifeless.

It is said that an art student can learn to "seduce" his or her right hand to more expressiveness by drawing with the left. Use of the left hand seems to release the right hand to greater freedom. Therapy for this woman, then, is to help impart new life to her thinking and, hence, her body, which had become as rigid, stiff, and unresponsive as her thinking. When she is free to express both sides of her nature, which we describe as her conservative and liberal sides, she will be more interesting to her husband and to herself.

This is not to say that conservatism means complete control and liberalism means complete license. Rather, when we use both eyes and both ears, we see and hear in depth. The actualizing person dances between the right and left complementary polarities, and in this process there is a natural restraint, rather than an artificial one, as demonstrated by our school teacher.

Suppose we regard our organism as a dynamic, ever-changing unit, yet bipolar in its potential for expression. We can see this more clearly in the form of a see-saw (Fig. 7).

A person in balance is one whose see-saw is moving continually in dynamic interplay between his or her conservative and liberal potentials. One side goes up, and that side comes into awareness; the needs of that side of nature dominate. Circumstances change, and the other end of the personal see-saw goes up. As long as we continue to live by the law of expression (expressing what we *feel* by behavior or verbal expression) then we will continue to be in balance. Neither the conservative nor the liberal tendencies will dominate or become fixed.

One of the basic needs of every person is to take responsibility for his or her own balance. Now here is the ethic we want to suggest: *Responsibility in this sense means accepting responsibility for oneself and one's own natural rhythmic balance, not depending on anyone else to establish controls for behavior.* We all have liberal and conservative sides. The conserva-

Figure 7

The Liberal/Conservative See-Saw

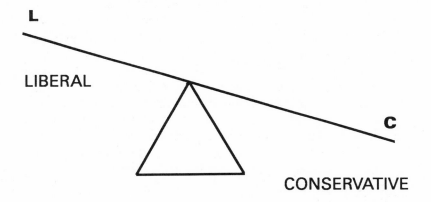

tive must accept her or his liberal side just as the liberal must accept her or his conservative side. In the open expression of both sides of one's nature, the individual has a natural means by which to live life with ease, combining challenge with a minimum of artificial controls imposed from the outside.

External systems of morality may be seen as blankets of artificial control required to keep immature people from behaving unwisely. As parents and spouses, we feel that we need to impose such systems on our children and our mates because, usually, we really do not trust our own balance and, therefore, cannot trust the balance of those we love.

An internal system of bipolar expression is, of course, the alternative to the external system of control. This has been described as a system of *organismic self-regulation*. Instead of simply controlling or braking one's natural expression, one focuses instead on an understanding of one's potentialities. Perls writes:

> I have still to see a case of nervous breakdown which is not due to over-control, and to its aggravation by the nagging of friends to "pull yourself together." The example of a car suggests itself. The car has many controls. The brakes are only one of them, and the crudest at that. The better the driver understands how to handle all the controls, the more efficiently will the car function. But if he drives with the brakes permanently on, the wear and tear on the brake and engine will be enormous . . . and sooner or later there will be a breakdown. . . . The overcontrolled person behaves in exactly the same way as the ignorant driver. He knows no other means of control than the brakes— than repressions.[1]

The actualizer, then, is someone who, aware of both his or her strengths and weaknesses, therefore does not project either of them excessively onto others. He or she is aware that there is always a parallel between how we feel about ourselves and how we feel about others. The manipulator, on the other hand, excessively fixated or preoccupied with her or his own strengths or weaknesses, denies or disowns those parts that she or he cannot accept.

For example, the manipulative businessman admits to his therapist that he has strong sexual desires for his secretary. Projecting his inner conservative self—his conscience and feelings of restraint—onto his wife, he secretly blames her for his dilemma. If the businessman were in therapy, the therapist might ask him to express both his liberal and his conservative views on this issue.

Therapist: Be your inner feelings about this.

Businessman: *I want that woman, and I don't care what it costs.*

Therapist: Okay. Now be your conservative feelings.

Businessman: *I don't have any conservative feelings.*

Therapist: I think you do. Wait for your conservative self to talk.

Businessman: (Long pause) *Hmmm. Well I guess it says, "Are you sure you would pay any price?"*

Therapist: And what does the liberal side say to that?

Businessman: *"Well, almost any price, so long as I don't hurt anybody."*

Therapist: And the conservative side?

Businessman: *What makes you think you won't hurt anybody? Especially yourself?*

Therapist: The liberal answer to that?

Businessman: *The liberal side says, "I guess there's always some kind of price."*

The dialogue could be continued, but our purpose is to show that the actualizing person is one who takes, embraces, and accepts ownership of his or her internal polarity while the manipulator projects and blames others. Let's look next at a college student who wants to drop out of school against his father's wishes.

Student: *I get so damned mad at my father's always demanding that I stay in school.*

Therapist: Let's pretend your father is sitting over there. Now tell me what he would say.

Student: *He'd say, "You'll never get a decent job if you quit school."*

Therapist: And you say?

Student: *I'm going in the army anyhow. Why can't I have some fun until I do?*

Therapist: And Father says?

Student: *"You dont' know how soon you're going into the army. You could use the time you have to learn as much as you can."*

Therapist:	And you say?
Student:	*You always want me to work and never let me have fun.*
Therapist:	Father says?
Student:	*"I want you to work so you can have fun."*
Therapist:	Who really said that? Your father or you?
Student:	*. . . I don't believe this! (Student becomes aware that the father he projected "out there" is really his own inner feeling of conservatism.)*

THE ROLE OF RELIGION

A word needs to be said here about the place of religion in guiding human behavior.[2] The practice of a religion is much like every other human endeavor. Some people practice their religious beliefs with manipulation, others practice their beliefs with more actualizing qualities. A manipulative practice stresses the human inability to trust in our own inner resources. An actualizing practice stresses that the kingdom of God is within each person, and that to trust one's inner self is to trust God's handiwork. The role of religion in the actualized sense is to foster self-direction and self-growth and to fulfill interpersonal relationships. Thus the actualizing priest, minister, or rabbi is seen by the actualizing person as less a judge and answer-giver and more as a resource person, one who shares and grows with his or her parishioners. He or she is a consultant, not a junior god.

The Manipulators

We believe that a good way to sum up this discussion of ethics is with a message from a poet with an introspective turn of mind.

Within my earthly temple there's a crowd;
There's one of us that's humble, one that's proud,
There's one that's broken-hearted for his sins,
And one that unrepentant sits and grins;

There's one that loves his neighbors as himself,
And one that cares for naught but fame and pelf,
From much corroding care I should be free
If I could once determine which is me![3]
(Edward Stanford Martin, "Mixed")

An actualizing person knows the two "crowds" within and willingly accepts each in the integrative fellowship of self.

NOTES

1. Frederick Perls, *Ego, Hunger and Aggression* (London: George Allen and Unwin, 1947), p. 224.
2. The whole idea of manipulation and actualization in religion is explored at greater length with two ministers, Maxie Dunnam and Gary Herbertson, in *The Manipulator and the Church* (Nashville: Abingdon Press, 1968). Also see Everett L. Shostrom and Dan Montgomery, *God in Your Personality* (Nashville: Abingdon Press, 1986).

III. Polarities and Growth

CHAPTER 12

Pleasing and Placating vs. Love: The Case of Arthur

How can it be bad to love?

It is not bad to love. Yet, there can be subtle distortions of this basic dimension of human experience that make love just another trick in the bag of manipulation. Consider the story of Arthur, who decided at some point in his life that his self was not sufficient to deal with conflict. He would do just about anything to avoid it. Out of his fear, he became a "pleaser and placater." He exaggerated his loving feelings, wanted everyone to be happy and tried heroically to meet everyone's needs. His emotional stance became so habitual that Arthur found himself nodding his head in agreement with everything anyone said. But the manipulative paradox was that Arthur seldom really listened to what anyone was saying. The act of appearing to be loving and agreeable distorted his true caring.

And Arthur was in a continual state of dissatisfaction. He never seemed to get sufficiently loving responses from others. No one seemed to care about his needs. On occasion, he would even encounter hostile opposition from others, no matter how much loving energy he expended on them. "Life isn't fair," he thought to himself. "I've *never* done anything against anyone else, so why should anyone be so rotten to me?" In his frustration, the usually super-nice Arthur would have occasional, unexplained outbursts of unreasonable anger.

The story of his life was simple: Whatever he did, he did so people would love him.

Arthur hated the boredom and discipline of school, but to please his parents and to avoid conflict with them, he studied hard, made A's, and graduated with honors. His father died when Arthur was in his late teens. Wanting more than ever to please his mother, Arthur went to college. She wanted him to be a teacher, but he wanted to be a sculptor.

"A sculptor?" she wailed when he told her of his dream. "Whoever heard of such a thing? Look in the want ads. In all of the state, is anybody looking for sculptors? It's teachers, teachers they're crying for. The work is clean; it's honest; it's professional. Be a good boy, Arthur. Be a teacher."

He became a teacher, reasoning that he could study his art in college and teach it when he finished, pleasing himself and his mother at the same time. Conflict would be avoided. The plan might have worked, except for one thing: He hated teaching. He found school more boring as a teacher than he ever had as a student. The pay was poor, and after a full day of dragging himself through the work he hated, Arthur had little enthusiasm for pursuing his own art.

Besides sculpture, Arthur had a talent for drawing, so he quit teaching and took a job as an illustrator in an advertising agency. Soon he was an art director with his own office, secretary, and printed business cards. One Saturday, he took his mother to his office to show her how well he was doing. She was impressed by the big desk and the carpeting, but said, "Anyway, it's too bad you left teaching. There, you were a professional."

So he went back to college and took a degree in architecture. The field promised everything he (and his mother) wanted: a chance to work with shapes, structures, and real materials, and most of all, the status of a "professional." His mother would surely be proud.

Arthur had married and had a good job and income, but for Arthur, everything seemed wrong—drastically wrong. He was thirty-two-years old and in good health; yet, he felt that his life was over. He had grown too fond of the wine he drank in ever-larger amounts each evening. He found a certain amount of satisfaction in his work, but there was no joy in it, no life. He began to feel that he had been cheated. "Please people," he had believed, "and they will love you." "Don't fight and argue with others," he maintained, "and they will love you." "Love is the key to happiness," he thought.

Arthur went out of his way to please people. He loaned people money. He helped them in business. Arthur was a really nice guy. Yet, for all his willingness to please, to love and be loved, Arthur was miserable. Arthur finally went into group psychotherapy. His wife had urged him to try it.

A TRANSFORMING EXPERIENCE

In the group, Arthur was open, communicative, and willing to please. Some of the group members liked his congenial ways, but others found him to be bland and somewhat irritating. His "niceness" was something of a burden. But whenever the subject of his art came up, he became animated and especially talkative.

"If you enjoy sculpting so much," Pat said, "why don't you do it for a living?"

"Oh, I've thought about it a lot," Arthur replied, "but it is hard to make a living as a sculptor. Art is a subjective thing, and it's hard to do something that will please enough people to make the work marketable."

"That's ridiculous," snarled Jim, a group member who found Arthur irritating. "You can't please everybody."

The therapist interrupted Jim's mounting tirade, "Arthur, I think it's time you have the experience of pleasing everyone! And I think your sculpture would be an ideal medium for the experience. Want to try it?"

"Why, sure!" he replied.

"All right. I'd like to commission you to do a bust of me. Do it in clay, so you can easily change it. When you get it done, bring it to group so we can get everyone's okay on it. Let's just see if you can please everyone!"

Arthur was pleased with the opportunity to show off his skill and with the prospect of pleasing his new friends in the group. He bought some clay and visited his model, the therapist, every Saturday. He worked with enthusiasm.

In a few weeks the bust was completed. With great ceremony, Arthur unveiled it for the group—and waited breathlessly for the group's reaction. The therapist was quite pleased at the results and told him so. Most of the others did the same. Only Martha was not pleased with it. "The brow is too heavy," she said. "It makes him look like he's brooding or gloomy. That's not his personality at all."

"You're right; you're right," Arthur agreed immediately. "I don't know how I could have done such a thing. I must fix it."

And he did. The next week, the eight-inch tall sculpture looked even more like the therapist, with the "heavy" brow corrected. Once again, most of the group members expressed their pleasure. Except Howard, who shook his head and said, "Now he looks pop-eyed. When you raised the brow, you took away the intellectual feel of the whole face."

Regarding the statue carefully, Arthur agreed. But Pat said the face shouldn't be too intellectual. She wanted the face of the statue to reflect the boyish innocence she saw in the real face of the therapist. Arthur agreed to that, too.

After some discussion, it was agreed that if just one person in the group was dissatisfied, the bust was not right, so Arthur took it home for more work. The next week, he unveiled it for the third time. Everyone agreed that the face of the statue was sufficiently intellectual with the appropriate trace of boyish charm. Everyone seemed to be totally pleased, until Donna said, "The more I look at the statue, the more upset I get about the chin. The chin is too sharp. You've made him look like a drill sergeant!"

"It doesn't have to look *exactly* like him, Donna," Arthur replied sharply. "This is a work of art, you know, so it contains some digressions from total reality."

"I'm no art expert," Donna retorted. "But I know what I like and what I don't like. I don't like that chin. It's not real. It's not him."

Reluctantly this time, Arthur agreed to rework the chin. But it was obvious that he didn't like the idea. When he unveiled it the fourth time, it was with none of the enthusiasm he had shown earlier. As before, most everyone liked what they saw. But Jim, after many moments of silence said, "To be perfectly honest with you, Arthur, that damn statue looked best the first time around. Every time you change it, it gets worse!"

"Well there's nothing I can do about it," Arthur replied with obvious irritation.

"Yes, you can," Jim said. "Just change it back to the way it was."

"No! Then the brow will be too heavy again," Martha shouted.

But Jim was adamant. "You certainly can't leave it the way it is. Be a sport. Give it another try."

Finally, Arthur exploded, "What in the hell is with you people? What does a guy have to do to please you, anyway? No matter what I do, it's not good enough! What do you want from me?"

"What do you want from *us*, Arthur?" the therapist asked.

"I want you to like this damned little statue. Is that too much to ask?"

"Most of us do like it," the therapist said.

"But the idea was for *all* of you to like it. That was the deal. That was what you said," Arthur wailed.

"What I said," the therapist replied, "is that we would find out if you *could* please everybody. It seems to be very important to you that absolutely everyone likes it. What does it mean to you if everyone doesn't?"

"It obviously means they don't like. . . ."

"They don't like you? Is that what it means?"

"This isn't fair," Arthur screamed. "I feel like I've been tricked and betrayed. I've worked hard to please you people, and what do I get? Tricked! I've had enough of all of you. I'm leaving and hope I never see any of you again."

"I understand how you feel, Arthur," the therapist said. "You have invested a great deal of yourself in this project, and I think you deserve a resolution. We've gone this far, Arthur, Are you willing to stick with us and see it through? Not for me, not for the others, but for you?"

"All right, I'll stay. But you made me damn angry. I'm sorry I went off like that. I usually don't act that way."

"I know," the therapist said. "You seem to have a very high tolerance level for frustration—maybe too high. And that may be part of the problem."

"Yeah," Jim said. "It gets a little nauseating the way you keep trying to please everyone all the time. It's just not real."

"I just want people to like me," Arthur said. "What's wrong with that? A person has to be liked. He's got to live in society. He can't do that if he makes nothing but enemies."

"So you're saying it's absolutely necessary for everyone to like you?" Martha said.

"Well, I certainly don't want people hating me."

"Do you want them loving you?" the therapist said.

"Of course."

"All of them? Everyone?"

"I don't see what's so wrong about that. I mean, it *is* something to shoot for."

"Arthur, have you ever heard of an election in this

country in which a candidate got every single vote?" asked the therapist.

"Uh, I suppose not."

"Have you ever seen a poll in which every person was either for or against one side, with no undecideds? Does that strike you as odd, Arthur? Is it surprising that not everyone loves one candidate or holds one point of view?"

"No, I guess it's only normal," Arthur admitted.

"So I guess you would have to say that it is only normal that some people are not going to like you. That not everyone is going to have your point of view. And that your point of view is as important as anyone else's," continued the therapist.

"I suppose so," Arthur conceded.

"I'm sure you know that intellectually, Arthur. But maybe you needed to *experience* it emotionally—in a safe setting—in a context that might have real meaning to you. I experience you as someone who really tries to avoid conflict and confrontation, who is afraid of anger and wants everyone to be happy, pleased, and loving. And you want to be always loving and lovable. Am I right?"

"Yes. I thought that was being a decent person. What's wrong with always being loving and lovable?"

"Nothing. It's just an impossible task. No one feels loving all the time. No one is lovable all the time. When you try to be, you are a phony— a manipulator—in your case a "pleasing and placating" manipulator. I suspect your experience here in group reflects a lot of your experience in your daily life. You try hard to be nice, loving, and pleasing, but the responses you get from others are less than you want and expect."

"You're right. That's the story of my life," Arthur mused.

"But you keep trying and trying until, finally, you get fed up and blow up."

"Yeah! Like I did tonight. Then I feel so guilty, like I've failed. I hate myself for days afterwards. I can't sleep. I can't forgive myself for being such a jerk. But I'm also damned angry at everyone else. I can't understand why everyone else is such a jerk, too."

"That's right. You feel bad because you haven't been honest to yourself about your feelings. Trying to please others all the time so they will like you and be under your control isn't love. It's manipulation. And asserting your rights, opinions, needs—confronting others and being willing to deal with conflict—isn't unloving. It's real. When you try to avoid conflict and confrontation—deny your anger—you are forced into a phony "pleasing and placating" role. Love and anger are just normal conditions of everyone's experience. Sometimes you are loving; sometimes you feel angry. When you avoid one, you force yourself into a manipulative role on the opposite polarity. You can diagram it this way:

LOVE ⎯⎯⎯⎯⎯⎯⎯⎯ ANGER

PLEASING & PLACATING

"When you deny your anger, you don't destroy it. You deflect it onto phony expressions of love. Arthur, your assignment, if you accept it, is to be an 'S.O.B.' for one week. Your wife is exempt, however, and no fisticuffs. Is there anything any of you want to add?"

"What are you going to do with the statue, Arthur?" Donna asked.

Arthur didn't reply. Raising both fists above his head, Arthur brought them down onto the clay, smashing it into a formless mass. "That's what I'm going to do with it," he roared with delight. "And when I start again—if I feel like starting again—I'm going to do it the way I damn well please. And if any of you don't like it, that's *your* problem."

Arthur was the most surprised person in the room when, spontaneously, everyone cheered.

CHAPTER 13

Blaming and Attacking vs. Anger: The Case of Mary

Love needs no defense. In its genuine expression, love is a natural, perhaps even a virtuous, impulse in an individual.

But anger? Anger is akin to sin, some believe. Many confuse anger with hate, with violent rage, with monumental destructiveness.

Yet, anger is as natural to the human as love is. Historically, collective anger has played a significant role in combatting injustice and establishing and safeguarding individual rights.

We may feel sorrow for the starving or abused child, but it is our anger that energizes us to do something about it. And the student who receives a low grade and the comment "poorly written" on an essay may feel hurt and defeated, but it is anger that energizes the student to "show that teacher what I can really do" on the next assignment.

The power and energy of anger that many of us fear and believe we must suppress is actually one of our

129

strongest motivators. Rather than suppressing and controlling anger, actualizers are able to direct the powerful emotion in ways that are enhancing to themselves and to their relationships with others.

ASSERTION

Honest expression of genuine anger is called assertion. Assertion is being able to confront others directly and truthfully. It is trusting yourself and others sufficiently to be able to face up to conflicts. Assertion is an antidote to rage, violence, and betrayal. It is the ability to recognize that the loud music on your co-worker's radio is making it difficult for you to concentrate (you are annoyed); that you can remedy the problem (eliminate the annoyance) with a direct, honest statement to the co-worker—"Would you mind turning off the radio? I'm having trouble concentrating"—and that you can confront another person as a fellow human being, not as an object to be avoided and feared.

Assertion simply requires three things:

1. Recognizing and acknowledging your genuine feeling of annoyance or anger.
2. Knowing you have the right to express that annoyance.
3. Trusting that the other person is capable of responding as a reasonable human being.

Manipulators are often so detached from their own feelings that they fail to recognize accurately and to acknowledge their feelings of annoyance. They feel miserable but are seldom able to name correctly the feeling or to perceive the reality surrounding their feelings. Instead, they see themselves as victims and others as enemies.

Mary, a rather lonely bookkeeper in a small manufacturing firm, was annoyed at her co-worker's loud radio. Mary hadn't tried to get to know her co-workers in the six months she had been working at Ely Tool and Die. But she had drawn her own conclusions about them and had decided none were worth the effort to befriend.

Betty, the young accounts payable clerk, had a desk less than six feet from Mary's. On her desk, Betty kept a small radio she enjoyed listening to on every afternoon.

Mary was annoyed. Instead of confronting Betty about the radio, Mary ruminated: "What's wrong with me? I'm such an idiot! I can't get these books to balance. Someone's liable to notice how long it's taking me to do this simple job. I bet that 'Brown-nose Betty' is just looking for an opportunity to make me look bad in front of everyone. I don't see how she gets away with having the radio on every afternoon. Why doesn't someone tell her to can it! She's so low-class, always acting *so* friendly with everyone—'Miss Popularity-Contest-Winner.' If I complained about the radio, everyone would side in with *her*."

Later, when break time arrived, Betty asked Mary if she would like to join her in the coffee room. In a screaming response that shocked even Mary, she said "I can't take a break! I haven't been able to finish this job thanks to you and your damned radio blasting in my ear all the time."

Mary shouldn't have been all that shocked at her outburst. She had been responding to others that way most of her adult life. As a sales clerk in a woman's shoe store, she disdained her co-workers and resented her boss. They didn't come up to her standards of how people should behave. But she seldom said much to them. Instead, she victimized her customers with sarcasm and ridicule. To a woman with an especially wide shoe size, she snarled, "You might try the army surplus store down the street."

As a student at a community college, she despised her teachers. "If they were any good, they wouldn't be teaching in this asylum," she thought. "Who do they think they are, anyway? They have no right to judge me." She left before the semester ended, but not before announcing to her English composition teacher, "Those who can 'do,' those who can't 'teach.'"

Mary was always leaving something. She was twenty-nine, had lived in three states, and had held more than ten jobs. She left home at seventeen, right after high school. She couldn't wait to get away from her violent, alcoholic father, her sickly mother, her five irritating brothers and sisters and the poverty, despair, and fundamentalist restraints that permeated her small midwestern hometown.

Her father was a very religious man. He demanded that his children attend Sunday school and church every week, Bible study every Wednesday night, and in Mary's case, choir practice every Thursday. And if they didn't, he beat the hell out of them.

Mary resented the enforced religiosity but was more terrified of the beatings. Even compliance didn't always save her from her father's arbitrary wrath when he had been drinking. She learned to keep quiet and to stay out of his way as much as possible.

Church, in spite of her upbringing, had been the one anchor in her life. But even church was a disappointment to her. She would go to one church for a while until someone said or did something she disapproved of, and then she would try another church until the same thing happened. It was through the church that she formed a few friendships, however temporary, and had a bit of social life, however superficial.

Mary's most self-nourishing activity was reading. She had read voraciously from childhood, mostly fiction and mystery stories. Lately, however, she had started to read self-help books in psychology and got the idea to enter therapy. She joined the group we met in the preceding chapter.

Like most new group members, Mary was reticent. She offered little information about herself and shared none of her feelings. In contrast to her reticence about herself and her small, rather delicate physique, Mary was—at least during the first three meetings she attended—pugnacious or, more accurately, cautiously belligerent, attacking and withdrawing. When she didn't show up for the fourth meeting, the group therapist called her.

"I don't think any of *you* can help *me*. Those people are the most screwed-up misfits I've ever seen," she explained.

"You may be right!" the therapist said. "But they are there to help one another, and it seems to be working for many of them. Maybe you have something to offer to the group as well. Maybe the group has something to offer you."

"The only thing I could offer is to tell them how messed up they are," Mary argued. "If I told them what I *really* thought of them, they'd probably all gang up on me."

"Does that make you afraid?"

"Yeah," she said after some thought. "They'd all stick together against me."

"What could they do to you?" the therapist asked.

"Well, nothing much, I guess. Maybe nothing at all."

"Will you come again? Will you tell them just what you think of them? Let's see if they can take it."

Mary agreed. The day arrived, and Mary was late.

"Welcome back, Mary. I'm glad you came. Would you mind if I share what we talked about on the phone last week with the group?" the therapist asked.

"Be my guest," she said testily.

"Well, Mary expressed some reservations about how much this group could help her," the therapist reported. "She explained that she felt critical about the group, but was afraid to express her criticisms. Being new to the group, she was afraid you might resent the things she might say," the therapist explained.

"I think she's afraid of what we might say to her," Jim sneered.

"You don't even know me! What could you possibly say to me?" Mary retorted.

"It's possible Mary could be afraid of that as well," the therapist interjected, "but let's stick to this one issue for now. Would any of you be willing to let Mary criticize you?"

"If she's got anything to say to me, I'd be willing to hear it," Donna announced in a small, but firm, voice.

"I'd feel terrible saying anything critical to you," Mary said brusquely. "You seem too fragile, like you'd faint if anybody even looked at you."

"I accept that, Mary," Donna responded. "I am timid and afraid, but I think I'm getting stronger."

"What about me?" Jim said. "Don't you have anything to say to me?"

"You remind me of my boss, 'Mr. Big Shot.' You think you're the only one with the right answer."

"Maybe you don't like the competition," cracked Jim.

Looking decidedly uncomfortable, Mary moved to the edge of her seat as if to escape. Arthur moved forward slightly and said, "Mary, I don't know much about you, but in spite of what you may think about me, I really would like to get to know you."

Mary blanched. Looking like a frightened, trapped animal, she raised herself half-way from the chair and froze, undecided whether to retreat back into the chair or to launch a frontal assault.

"I have an idea," the therapist said. "Mary, you are facing two people here—Jim, who is rather negative and aggressive toward you, and Arthur, who is expressing some caring for you. Do you feel the difference?"

Sinking back into her chair, Mary relaxed a bit and with a sigh of resignation said, "Not much. It feels about the same to me."

"Correct me if I'm wrong, but it looks as if you are afraid of contact with anyone, whether it's negative or positive contact," the therapist commented. "Does that statement feel right?"

Mary avoided looking at anyone and sat quite still for several minutes. Tears began to emerge from her half-closed eyes. She suddenly opened them and looked directly at Arthur first, then at Jim, and then at Arthur again, as if she were seeing them for the first time.

"I never thought about it that way, but I guess you're right. I wasn't seeing a difference. Everybody is just a threatening blob to me," Mary whispered.

"I think you've made an important discovery about yourself, Mary," the therapist said. "I think it's worth pursuing, and I believe there is more to discover if you are willing to risk it."

Mary continued in group therapy, and for several weeks she managed to keep the focus of the group off herself by showing an inordinate amount of interest, for her, in the other group members and their difficulties. She listened intently to what each person had to say and even managed to contribute a few supportive ideas. Fearing the group's attention, she choked back her usual acerbic remarks. The results, if not dramatic, were notable, even to Mary. During the week between group sessions, she would find herself thinking about the other group members *as if she cared about them.* She found it easier each week to chat with them before and after the sessions. She even began to look forward to group. In short, Mary was learning that she needed people.

Encouraged by her experiences with the therapy group, Mary had been indulging in pleasant little fantasies—of people walking up to her desk at the office to ask her advice, to tell her how wonderful she was; of crowds competing with one another for her attention. In her fantasies, she was always seated safely *behind* her desk as the admiring, faceless throngs worshiped her from the other side. But her reality was quite different. Her co-workers stayed at a safe distance, it's true, but none were admiring.

Mary was still having difficulty at work. The more she felt at ease in group therapy, the more alienated she felt at her job. For the first time, Mary recognized her aloneness, and it was painful. Her awkward attempts to join in with the other women at work were met with suspicion. Her lunch with the new file clerk, Joanne, had disappointed her. Joanne had not been particularly sympathetic with Mary's complaints about the unfair office rules, about "Mr. Big Shot" boss, or about "Brown-nose Betty."

Mary wanted friends, and at the same time she wanted to criticize those she would befriend. As miserable as she had been before therapy, she was even more miserable since. She was confused and desperate. Mary was entering a crisis in her life.

In any life a crisis is a turning point, an important event fraught not only with danger but also with immense possibility. in therapy, a crisis is called a breakthrough, a kind of "planned crisis," wherein clients begin to recognize and to abandon the "coping skills" (manipulations) that have served them, however poorly, throughout their lives. It's like changing into a new set of clothes. The old clothes are ragged and unsightly, worn too thin for real warmth, but they are comfortable in their familiarity, and they at least cover our nakedness. When we part with them, we feel naked and exposed, with no place to hide, until we can learn to fit into our new wardrobe. At least that's how it feels when we begin to change from manipulating to being real.

Mary literally ran to her next group session. She was desperate for the comfort of their caring. Breathless and panicky, and before the group members had even settled into their seats, Mary announced that the group must deal with her problem immediately.

A TRANSFORMING EXPERIENCE

"I feel so alone and afraid! I don't think anyone will ever care about me. I feel like I'm on a huge ocean, trapped alone in a small boat that will never, never make it to shore."

"Mary, I hear your despair and am moved by your description," the therapist responded.

"What's happened, Mary?" Arthur asked.

"I'm trying so hard now to make friends, but nothing seems to work," Mary cried "Everyone seems to want to keep me out of everything. Even the new girl at the office. I thought we could be friends, but she's just like the others."

"What's her name?" the therapist asked.

"What? Whose name?"

"The new girl you want to be friends with."

"Oh, uh, Joanne, I guess. But I think I'll start calling her 'Brown-nose Betty's Side-kick.' She seems to get along just great with her."

"And you feel left out, right?" Jim said.

"Yeah!"

"I've been curious, Mary," the therapist interjected. "Why do you always call Betty 'Brown-nose Betty' and your boss 'Mr. Big Shot'?

"Well, that's what they are!" Mary shot back defensively.

"To you."

"What do you mean 'to me?' That's what they are!":

"If that's what they are—all they are—they would be that to their mothers, fathers, spouses, children and friends. Do you think when your boss goes home to his family his children greet him with 'Hi, Mr. Big Shot'? Or Betty's husband says, 'What's cooking, Brown-nose Betty?'"

"Well, of course not," Mary answered amid the group's snickering laughter.

"I think we have hit on something here," the therapist said, "that might be a clue to something important. What do you think that is?"

Mary sat quietly for a while, trying to absorb what seemed utterly ridiculous. Finally she spoke, "I think I get what you're saying. I don't call them those names to their faces, of course, but that's how I've been seeing them. I haven't been able to see them as real human beings."

"That's right," the therapist said. "It's impossible to be friends with someone you define in such a reductive way. You can't be fully human with someone you see as less than fully human. You have been allowing your self only two choices in your relationships with others: seeing them as either objects to fear or objects to criticize. I'm really pleased at your insight, Mary.

"Also, I was interested in how you described your feelings of loneliness. 'Like being trapped in a boat that will never get to shore,' is how I think you described it. It reminds me of a poem called "The Rime of the Ancient Mariner," which has meant a great deal to me. The poem is a fantasy about a young sailor at sea who kills an albatross. The albatross, a bird that follows ships, is considered almost sacred in sailors' lore. This killing of the ship's 'sacred guest' leads to terrible misfortune. The winds that move the ship are calmed, and all the sailor's shipmates die. He is alone. His shipmates are dead to him, and the ship on which he is trapped drifts aimlessly with no wind to carry it back to shore. Is that how you feel, Mary?"

Sobbing, Mary sputtered, "Yes, and it's awful. I feel so hopeless."

"What happens to the sailor? Does he ever get back to shore?" Arthur questioned.

"Yes, he does," the therapist answered. "And this is the part that has meant the most to me, and maybe it will mean something to you, too, Mary. The sailor looks at the 'slimy creatures' swimming in the sea, the creatures he had been despising for their ugliness and their imperfections. But suddenly, out of his despair, he is able to see their beauty, and he says

A spring of love gushed from my heart
And I blessed them unaware

At that moment the spell is broken, a wind arises, the sails fill, and the ship begins to move.

"I think that's what I've been doing most of my life," Mary said. "I keep seeing everybody's imperfections, including my own, and judging everyone, not for what they really are, but for what *I* think they are. I used to hate people who go around seeing everything through rose-colored glasses, but I think I've been seeing everything through muddy lenses. But it's hard to change, and I'm not sure I can."

"You're right," the therapist said. "It is hard to change, and you shouldn't try to change everything all at once. Life doesn't have magic spells that can be broken with just one word. But like the sailor in the poem, you have in you the capacity to love and accept others just as they are, and even more important to love and accept yourself just as you are."

"Just stop calling everybody by your pet names," Jim snorted. And everyone laughed.

CHAPTER 14

Withdrawing and Avoiding vs. Weakness: The Case of Donna

The human being—

> . . . Placed on this isthmus of a middle state,
> A being darkly wise and rudely great:
> With too much knowledge for the Sceptic side,
> With too much weakness for the Stoic's pride,
> He hangs between; in doubt to act or rest
> Pope, "Know Thyself"

Only a fool believes that he or she is invulnerable, all-knowing, all-powerful. Weakness is a reality in each and every one of us. Awareness of our limitations helps us to plan, to use our intelligence to avoid crises, to meet challenges, and to direct our energies to the areas of our greatest strengths.

Humans, for example, have been yearning to fly for centuries, the bravest ones flinging themselves off cliffs with capes of feathers attached to their wildly flapping arms. Sad experience taught them that they were just too weak to fly, their strength and energy insufficient to defy the pull of gravity. Acknowledging that reality, of course, led to other possibilities, and now humans fly every day.

A young woman with talent in music and a great love for the opera, but who could not sing, would have been foolish to have devoted her life to becoming a mezzo soprano. To her credit, she recognized her limitations and became one of the more generous patrons of the opera.

These examples are obvious, but they contain one of life's great lessons: acknowledging our weakness is one of our greatest strengths.

Actualizers, with a heightened self-awareness, know their weaknesses and then act on the knowledge. They look for detours, ways around their limitations, solutions to their problems. If they are alcoholic, they do not drink. If they are blind, they learn Braille. If they are procrastinators, they create incentives.

Manipulators who fear strength and adequacy are clearly unaware of specific weaknesses in themselves, even though they often play "weak." To avoid resolve and responsibility (real strength), *withdrawers and avoiders* try to convince others of their general inadequacy. The tragedy is that they end up convincing themselves that they are inherently powerless and hopeless. Feeling miserable much of the time, they are characteristically ignorant of their own inner feelings. They tend to intellectualize, spout clichés, play "poor-me" roles, and seek from others what can be found only in themselves. To confront their real weakness would uncover their real strength. They rely instead on false bravado.

Donna had been an only child, born late in her parents' lives. Her parents were kind, decent people, not wealthy but financially comfortable.

Donna's mother was the perfect mother and homemaker. She kept an immaculate house, was a wonderful cook and did *everything* for Donna. Their home was always neat and clean, but Donna never dusted a table. Dinner was always on time, but Donna never peeled a potato or set a table. Whenever Donna would have a friend over to play, her mother allowed no games or activities that would mess things up. "No cookie baking by children in my kitchen," she would tell her daughter. Donna never had to do anything, and nothing was ever expected of her. She was her parents' pride and joy!

When Donna was in her junior year in high school, her father had a massive heart attack. He lived, but the medical expenses exceeded their insurance coverage, and they had to draw heavily on their savings. Just when Donna should have been enjoying the social joys of her teen years, her father was gravely ill, the family income had been drastically reduced, and her mother was breaking under the strain. Her mother needed, in fact demanded, her help. Donna's help, however, never seemed to satisfy her mother's expectations. They argued constantly, especially about money and Donna's inadequacy.

Desperate to help out her family and to prove herself, Donna decided to find a job. A neighbor who owned a diner on the nearby interstate highway hired her as a waitress. She was ill prepared for the demands of the job. The diner was a truck stop, and the truckers, always in a hurry, were impatient with her inexperience. Each night was a humiliation of wrong orders,

143

mistakes on checks, and spilled coffee. During her breaks, her cheeks still smarting from the rude insults of dissatisfied customers, Donna would hide in the dark storeroom, trying to gather her courage. After a time, Donna's work improved. She was catching on, but she was never able to shake the anxious feeling she got each time she reported for work.

Most of Donna's customers didn't bother to chat with her the way they did with the other waitresses, but she began to notice that one of the regulars was paying special attention to her. He was different, smaller and not as loud as the others. He asked her to call him Larry, and he always left her a larger tip than anyone else did.

One rainy morning, as Donna was leaving the restaurant, Larry was waiting for her. He offered her a ride home in his rig. Not knowing how to refuse, she scrambled into the high cab and rode with him back to the crossroads near her house. In the months that followed, he drove her home whenever he stopped at the restaurant. On one of these trips, he leaned over, kissed her, and asked her to marry him. She had just turned eighteen.

Donna hadn't dated much. She had imagined that no one would ever want her. Yet, here was Larry, ready to sweep her off her feet, take her away, and take care of her. She figured that her parents would be pleased. They weren't. But Donna married Larry anyway. They were wed at a small chapel in Las Vegas on the way to his apartment in Los Angeles.

At first she was lonely and lost in the big, strange city, but in time she had two baby boys to take care of. She grew accustomed to Larry's long absences and didn't know that other drivers did not stay away as long as her husband did, that when he was gone for fourteen days, his work took up only ten. But he took care of almost everything for her, leaving her free to enjoy her children.

As time passed, Larry began paying less attention to her sexually. He wouldn't kiss her or even touch her for months. This bothered her, not because she missed or craved the sex act, but because, to her, it meant she wasn't good enough. As a lover, Larry had always been abrupt and inattentive to her. Unsatisfying as their sexual relationship had always been for her, she nevertheless had felt reassured when he wanted her. She had not experienced that reassurance for two years.

She finally decided that Larry must be having an affair. He had to be "getting it somewhere else." For months she fought with herself about confronting him on the issue, but she could never muster the courage to ask.

One Friday evening, their six-year-old son was rushed to the hospital with appendicitis and needed immediate surgery. She felt frightened and unable to cope with her son's illness all alone. She tried to reach Larry, who was on the road. She called the depots where he was scheduled to make deliveries, but no one had seen him in days. Panic-stricken, she called the central dispatch office in Phoenix and was told that Larry had finished four days earlier and had told them he was going home.

When he did come the next day, she asked where he'd been. He said he'd made an extra side-run.

"You're lying," she spat out. "You're having an affair with another woman."

Larry sat back in his chair, sighed tiredly, and said, "You're only half right, Donna. I am having an affair, but not with a woman."

For a moment, she didn't understand. Then the realization hit her. She gasped.

"Ever since I was a teenager," he admitted quietly. "I thought that getting married would change me. It hasn't. I'm not interested in you—or any woman for that matter. Maybe it's just as well that it came out now. I was going to tell you sooner or later anyway. I'm sorry."

That weekend, he moved out and moved in with his lover. Every two weeks Larry sent her a check, but the money didn't begin to cover the cost of supporting Donna and her two sons. She tried her best to get office jobs, but she had few marketable skills. The most she could do was put her name on the lists of the temporary agencies. But the combination of her inexperience and lack of self-confidence kept her name at the bottom of the lists. She earned extra money by caring for children of working women in her home.

About that time the headaches and stomach cramps began. No amount of aspirin or antacid could make them go away. Doctors could find no apparent cause for her ailments, and finally one suggested that her illness might be "nerves." He recommended that she consult a psychologist, and she entered the therapy group.

A TRANSFORMING EXPERIENCE

In the first few sessions, it was difficult for Donna to talk. But in the fourth week, Pat, one of the group members, mentioned that she had a cold. This reference to illness seemed to bring Donna out a bit.

"I've been sick lately, too. I have headaches and stomach cramps, and the doctors can't find what's causing them. That's why I'm here, to see if it's all in my head. But listen to me, going on about my pains. I'm sorry. We should be talking about more important things."

"Not at all, Donna," the therapist interjected. "We can talk about whatever's on your mind."

"I really shouldn't have brought this up at all," she said, brushing imaginary lint from her black skirt. "It really is nothing. Almost nothing, anyway. I shouldn't let a few pains bother me. I've lived with them all these years. They're not worth mentioning."

"But you *did* mention them," the therapist reminded her.

"If I could just pull myself together, I'd be okay," she said. "Nothing can change the past. All I can do is just live with the problems now." Her eyes took on a look of brave, but hollow, hopefulness.

"What past do you want to change?" asked Arthur.

"My marriage, my husband, myself—just about everything," she answered.

"What about your marriage?" the therapist queried. "You are separated, I recall."

"Yes, for about two years now. Larry left me for a man," she blurted out. "I can't believe I didn't know, that I never suspected. I was so stupid. It's so humiliating. I should have been able to tell. If only I had known. . . . Now, I'm left with two children and not enough to support them. I'm sure I can make it, but it's awful hard. I'll have to grit my teeth, stand up to it, and walk through it," Donna said unconvincingly.

"That's nice to say, Donna," offered Pat, "but does

it relieve any of the pain or do anything about it?"

"It would if I could just pull myself together," she answered. "If I could just grow up and be adult about everything. I'm sure everything would be all right."

"You *are* an adult, Donna," the therapist said softly. "You are grown up and everything isn't all right, is it?"

Donna sighed and slouched back into the couch. "No, everything isn't all right. Not at all. The more I think about it, the worse I feel. Even now, I feel like a sick helpless old lady. Nothing seems to help. Not the medicines, not talking about it, not anything." Tears began to well in the corners of her eyes and spill down her cheeks. She made no effort to hide them or to wipe them away.

The therapist walked over to her and put his hand on her arm and said, "if you don't mind, Donna, I'd like to try something that might help a little bit. It's a process called 'focusing.'¹ It was developed by Eugene Gendlin, a psychology professor in Chicago. Actually it's designed to be something you can do yourself, but I'd like everyone to see it just once so they can all try it."

"I'm willing to try it," Donna said resignedly.

"All right," the therapist began. "Take a few deep breaths. Close your eyes if you want to." She did as he suggested.

"Ready? Now, first of all I would like you to make a little space for yourself. Just push all your thoughts and everything else away a little. Then start paying attention to your body. Just think about how your body feels. Focus on the pit of your stomach. Got it?"

"Yes."

"Good. Now see what happens there when you say this: 'Everything would be okay except for . . . ' and think of one or two problems that are bothering you.

Just let the problems come up. Don't try to go inside them right now. Stand back. Leave a little space between you and them. This is called 'making a space.' Are you able to do that?"

She seemed a little surprised: "Yes, I am."

"Great. Now pick one problem to focus on, the most significant one you feel in your body. If you've got it, tell me what it is."

"It's all that stuff about Larry."

"That's fine. Don't think about it right now. Just get a sense of what it feels like. Is it like a taste, a musical chord, a big weight, or what? Don't answer yet. You needn't get involved with words, just the feeling of the whole thing, even if it's unclear."

The therapist waited a moment for her to get in touch with this "felt sense."

"It's just this big, fuzzy feeling," she said.

"See if a word comes to mind that matches that whole thing about Larry, that 'felt sense.' Is it tight? Sticky? Heavy? Maybe it's a phrase or a mental image. Is anything like that coming up?"

"Yes. It's like a twisting. That's it: a big, twisting feeling, going right through my middle," she said with a little sigh.

"When you say *twisting*, does something happen to that feeling? Does it change a little?"

"Yes, it eased a little. It let up, sort of."

"That's a good sign. But does the word *twisting* completely match that unclear thing about Larry?"

She sat quietly for several minutes.

"Wait a minute. The word is changing. It's like I'm screwed, screwed to the wall . . . not exactly screwed, though, more like . . . pinned! That's it, pinned to the wall! That feels right. It feels horrible, but it feels right,

or true. Know what I mean?" She heaved a tremendous
sigh.

"Stay with the word *pinned*," the therapist urged.
"Keep testing the word *pinned* against that feeling in
your stomach, all about Larry. Ask questions like 'What
is it about the problem that makes me feel *pinned*?' Ask
and *wait* for the answer. Don't try to answer it
yourself."

She sat quietly again for several moments. Her
forehead wrinkled a little, and her legs began to twitch.
She involuntarily shrugged her shoulders.

"Stay with it," the therapist urged. "Keep asking until
you receive something." Her shoulders shrugged more
and tears began forming at the edges of her closed
eyelids. She was experiencing what Gendlin calls a
"body shift."

"What are you receiving?" the therapist asked.

"Helplessness," she said flatly. Her breaths were
short and her voice sad. "Total helplessness. I'm stuck
with Larry, and there's nothing I can do."

"All right, you've had a shift, and you've gotten an
awareness. Be with that for a few moments. Experience
the feeling of helplessness some more. Just keep
experiencing that feeling of helplessness, okay?"

"Okay."

All of the group watched and waited. After a minute
or two had gone by, the therapist asked, "Anything you
can tell us about the feeling?"

"You know, all that talk I gave you earlier, about
gritting my teeth and walking through it? It sounded
good, but it didn't really *feel* right. This feeling of
helplessness is real."

"Donna, ask your body what is real about this
helplessness. Don't try to answer yourself. Just wait

until something comes up," the therapist said.

The group members waited quietly, hardly breathing.

"I'm not going anywhere in my life, and that's for real. I feel like I'm hung in limbo. Between nothing and nothing. Time is going by without anything to distinguish one day from another," she said.

"What's the worst thing about that limbo?" the therapist asked.

"That I'll live to be a very old lady, and when I finally die the most remarkable thing anyone could say about me is that I stayed married to a man who couldn't love me! Oh my! I just realized something. It isn't that Larry doesn't love, or won't love me. He just *can't* love me!"

"What does that feel like?"

She sighed audibly. "It feels like an immense relief, like I just floated free. Like I just pulled out the pin all by myself. Like I'm not so helpless after all."

"Good. Let's take this one more step, Donna, and I want you to stay with the feeling in your body. Don't try to figure out anything. Just wait for the answer. Ask your body what it feels like *not to be helpless after all*," the therapist said.

The group had never been so quiet or so involved. After many moments, Donna said, "It feels breezy."

The tension in the group exploded into laughter. Looking anxiously for Donna's reaction to the mirth, Arthur started to hush the group, fearing she would be offended. But what he saw was a radiant smile. "Breezy?" Arthur queried. "You feel breezy?"

"Yes. It seems ridiculous, but that is exactly what it feels like. A cool, clean, luscious wind inside and out. I feel almost like I am a part of the wind. I feel as if I can go anywhere, do almost anything. It's a great feeling,"

Donna said. "I don't think I've ever felt quite that way before. You know, I have a lot of problems I don't know exactly how to deal with, and it's scary, but right now I feel as though I can face them. I feel that I'll be okay. I am okay!"

This focusing experience helped Donna to do what actualizing people do: to experience herself, and herself as a part of her world, more wholly and accurately. Manipulators experience themselves fragmentally. They compartmentalize themselves into brain (thinking), emotion (feeling), and physical (body). Manipulators try to explain everything intellectually, ignoring the emotional pain in their bodies as if it were something separate from themselves. Actualizers, on the other hand, experience themselves wholly. They know that the body is where emotion is felt, and they are attentive to their bodily feelings. They allow their bodies, feelings, and thoughts to work together.

Before Donna's focusing session, she had been using the manipulator's approaches to a problem. In Gendlin's book, *Focusing*, they are called belittling the problem, analyzing, facing down the feeling, lecturing yourself, and drowning the feeling.[2]

Belittling the problem. This is what Donna was doing when she said, "It really is nothing. . . . I shouldn't let a few pains bother me." Such an approach will get you nowhere. If pains are important enough for your body to feel, they're important enough to look into, get inside of, and get clear. In fact, by pushing it aside, you probably make it worse.

Analyzing. Donna was analyzing when she said, "I can't believe I didn't know, that I never suspected. . . . I was so stupid. . . . If only I'd have known." Your analysis may or may not be correct, but it won't make the feeling in your gut, with its inexplicable discomforts and tensions, go away.

Facing down the feeling. Again, when Donna said, "I'll have to grit my teeth, stand up to it, walk through it," she sounded courageous and noble, but she actually showed false bravado. This is just an intellectual exercise and does nothing to change the situation or the feelings.

Lecturing yourself. In Donna's words, "If I could just grow up and be adult about this, I'm sure everything would be all right." This doesn't work either. It's based on the mistaken notion that adults don't have feelings, or that they don't have a right to feelings. Lecturing yourself is just piling guilt on top of your problem, and guilt just makes it worse.

Drowning the feeling. Donna indulged in this when she slouched back into the couch and said, "The more I think about it the worse I feel. . . . I feel like a sick helpless old lady." She was right, sinking into the bad feeling only reinforces it and makes you feel worse.

In the focusing session, Donna learned something about experiencing the reality of her feelings and owning up to the reality of her circumstances. When she was able to do this and quit playing the role of the helpless one, a wide spectrum of long hidden feelings and long missed opportunities began to emerge.

NOTES

1. See Eugene T. Gendlin, *Focusing,* (New York: Everest House Publishers, 1978).
2. Ibid., pp. 39-40.

CHAPTER 15

Controlling and Dictating vs. Strength: The Case of Gary

Strength and weakness are extreme opposites—or so they seem. Yet, life experience demonstrates the paradoxical nature of the polarity that *in weakness is strength* and *in strength is weakness*. This polarity is like two sides of the same coin: Slice a coin in half, and each slice still has both sides.

Controlling and *dictating* manipulators, however, denying this reality, futilely try to divide and conquer their own weakness, destroying in the process their genuine strength.

Genuine strength, on one side, is to endure, to persevere, and to survive. Its qualities are adequacy, self-esteem, and self-reliance. On the other side, genuine weakness is to be vulnerable, to be open, and to be interdependent. Its qualities are trust, honesty, and cooperation.

Inordinately fearful of helplessness, hurt, and humiliation, manipulators try to recreate themselves into invulnerable fortresses, totally self-contained.

Never certain of their success, however, they try to disarm others, negating the power in everyone else. Not trusting others, they cannot acknowledge or tolerate strength in anyone but themselves.

Gary was that kind of manipulator.

Life should have been easy for the bright, good-looking boy. His family was, by most standards, wealthy. His father, a prominent surgeon in an affluent area of southern California, had provided his wife and son with a large beautiful home, swimming pool, expensive cars, and designer clothes. Gary's father was a respected and powerful man in his community, and Gary idolized him. Wanting to grow up to be just like his father, Gary studied hard in school. He was determined to always be at the head of his class, just like his father. Always in control, just like his father.

But Gary seldom saw his father, who would leave for hospital rounds before the family was up and was seldom home before Gary's bed time. Gary knew his father best through the scrapbook of newspaper clippings Gary had been collecting since he was eight—articles about new surgical procedures his father had developed, about his father's trips to disaster stricken Third World countries as a member of medical teams, about his father's appointment as chief of staff.

Gary didn't see much of his mother, either, not because she wasn't home. She seldom was up to get Gary ready for school in the mornings, and after school Gary would often find her still in bed or asleep on the couch. She told him she didn't feel well.

When Gary was ten, he heard his parents arguing, something they seldom did. His father's voice was angry. The house, he complained, was in constant disarray, dishes piled in the sink most of the time. Gary heard his mother defend herself, "I need more help. It's hard raising a child all by myself. You're never here to see what it's like," she wailed. Within a couple of days, a housekeeper arrived. She came every morning, and order began to be restored. But Gary's mom remained much the same.

One day Gary overhead the housekeeper gossiping with a friend over the phone: "The woman's a real lush, I tell you. If it weren't for peanut butter and jelly sandwiches, I think this kid would have starved to death before I came." When he realized who she was talking about, he felt a tremendous, hot humiliation spread throughout his body. His mind raced. His mother was a drunk, that's what she meant. How many people had she told this to? Did his father know?

Gary knew what he had to do. He had to get the housekeeper fired. He had to protect his mother. He had to protect his father. He had to take charge.

By the time Gary was twelve, he had become quite adept at taking care of the house and his mother when she "didn't feel well." There were longer periods of time between his mother's drinking bouts, but he could never be sure of her. On important occasions when he would plan to have friends over, he could never be sure his mother would be in a condition to receive company. Sometimes she kept her promise not to drink, and all was well. At other times, he would find her passed out on the floor just in time to divert a friend from tripping over her. He could never count on her, so he learned to develop contingency plans when she let him down.

As far as Gary could tell, his father didn't realize the extent of his wife's drinking problem. Gary didn't want his father to be worried about things that Gary could take care of. Gary believed he was doing a good job. He and his mother had entered into a kind of conspiracy to cover up her problem. To outsiders, he thought, everything looked normal. He made sure that meals were prepared, and that the house was clean and orderly. He even made excellent grades in school. Gary was a very strong child, and the family was still together.

By the time Gary was in college, however, his parents had separated. And by the time he graduated and entered medical school, they had divorced. His parents' separation was a serious blow to him.

His frequent visits with his mother surprised him. She seemed to be recovering from her alcoholism, or else she was just "dried out" in honor of his visits, he would say to himself. He could never be sure. He couldn't really trust her. He felt concerned about her, living alone.

When Gary finally finished medical school, he was anxious to move ahead rapidly, to join ranks with his father, but his internship and residency seemed to drag on forever. And the work was demanding. He had to give up much of his self-appointed supervision of his mother and her problems, and months went by without contact from his father. He tackled the grueling, long hours of his residency with the same zeal he had tackled everything else in his young life, refusing to admit to anyone, even himself, how exhausted he was. He volunteered for extra hours beyond the impossibly long shifts of his regular assignments. The other residents thought he was crazy, but they were glad for the chance of an hour or two of rest when he offered to fill in for them.

Gary didn't want to miss anything that might keep him ahead of the rest. He thought he was the best of the residents. In fact, he thought he could teach most of the doctors in the hospital a thing or two.

Gary was lucky. When his over-confidence and exhaustion caused him to miscalculate a dosage on a patients's prescription, a young nurse named Jennie caught his error in time. He was both grateful and angry—angry with himself for his mistake, and angry with her for knowing about it. He had found her attractive and had planned to ask her out when his residency was finished. Now he wasn't so sure.

But she was. She had been watching him in both awe and horror. She was astonished and impressed by his total dedication, at the same time almost holding her breath, waiting for the disaster she was sure would follow. When she was able to help him over it, the bond between them was sealed—for her. Here was a man she wanted, a man headed for the top of his profession. She wanted to be with him, to help him get there.

And she knew he had been watching her, too. But now his "watching" had taken on a new character. He was surly and demanding, checking up on her work, looking for mistakes he seemed sure *she* was making. After many angry encounters between them, she finally told him she wanted to talk with him in "neutral territory." She suggested they meet for coffee away from the hospital. He declined.

"Listen to me," Jennie demanded. "You owe me an explanation. You've been on my back for weeks now, and I know I don't deserve it."

Gary finally relented. They met at an all night coffee shop after her shift. He apologized to her, explaining how important his medical career was to him. "I can't take any chances that some nurse is going to screw up my orders and make me the fall guy."

"Screw up *your* orders," she responded coolly. "As I recall, you screwed up all on your own." Then with more warmth she said, "But it can happen to the best doctor in the world when he's working eighteen-hour shifts day after day. I have great respect for you. I think you are one of the best doctors, or will be."

That was what he wanted to hear. He wanted her admiration very much at this moment. They continued talking until he was almost late getting back to his next shift. He told her all his dreams and plans, and she seemed as interested in them as he was.

They saw each other regularly, and within a few months, he asked her to marry him. Then their conflicts began all over again. She wanted to continue her career so they could work together. He wanted her to quit even before they were married.

"It costs money to start a medical practice, and it costs money to live. We need my income," Jennie argued.

"Your income is nothing," Gary shouted. "I don't need your income. It wouldn't even keep us in toothpaste! Besides, wives of professional men don't work. It's demeaning."

"I'm a professional, too," Jennie responded with hurt in her voice.

"You don't look very professional. You look like a kid just out of braces. And why can't you do something about your hair?" he replied sarcastically.

"What's wrong with my hair?" Jennie screamed.

"Nothing, if you were a co-ed, but it's time you graduated. I need a wife with some elegance. Your wardrobe looks like hippie cast-offs."

Then he got up off the couch as if to make a speech: "*I* can take care of *my* career, and *I* can take care of *my* money. I want my wife to take care of herself."

"Your money? Is that how it is? *Your* career? Am I going to be just another possession for showing off? That's not what *I* want. I want to be your wife, to help you and be with you. I need some respect, too, and I need to be needed."

Gary really wanted Jennie, but she kept resisting his carefully laid plans for his life. The harder he tried to make her understand, the more stubborn she became. He was having problems with his career, too, but he couldn't share them with her. He was sure he would lose her if she knew the difficulties he was having getting as much money as he needed from the bank to start his practice.

Everything had been going well until he went to the bank for the final interview with the loan officer. The bank had approved a certain amount, but he knew he would need more to get the quantity and quality of equipment and furnishings he needed for his office, and for the six months of salaries for the staff he knew would be necessary. The loan officer kept arguing with him as if he knew more about a medical practice than Gary did.

By the end of the frustrating meeting, the loan officer had withdrawn the original offer, and Gary was stunned. Feeling miffed and humiliated, Gary immediately scheduled an appointment with the bank president, but the earliest time available was a week away.

On his way to see his mother one afternoon, he planned his strategy, rehearsing what he would say to the bank president when he finally got in to see her. He decided to practice his speech in front of his mother. She was easier to talk to now than she had been when he was a child. She seemed to really listen and to care about him these days. He didn't want to worry her—he wouldn't tell her how bad it was. He'd tell her he was going in for his first interview for the loan. At the conclusion of his performance for his mother, she asked if Jennie was going with him to the interview.

"Why should she go?" he asked.

"Oh, I just thought she might be of help. You two are getting married next month, and I'm sure this matters a great deal to her as well."

"Well, I'm not so sure we're getting married at all," Gary blurted out before he could stop himself. "I'm not sure of anything right now. She is so stubborn. She won't listen to reason."

Gary found himself confessing all his problems to his mother. It was quite a role reversal. He had spent years parenting her, protecting her, and now he was parading all his fears in front of this weak, pathetic woman.

"I think things will be just fine for you, Gary," his mother said, "But I've been thinking about how much responsibility you've had to carry all alone since you were a young child. I feel so sorry about it, but I want you to know how much I care for you and appreciate your strength. I want to do something for you now, but I must have your promise that you'll accept it before I tell you what it is."

With much puzzlement and some protestation, Gary finally promised. To his extreme surprise, she said, "I want you to join a therapy group. I'll pay. It isn't much expense, but I think you'll get something out of it, perhaps something your father and I wanted for you, but were never able to provide. You're so used to taking care of everything yourself, Gary, but I think it's time you found out that others have something to offer."

Gary kept his promise.

A TRANSFORMING EXPERIENCE

Gary was very willing to talk in group. He explained that he was there only to please his mother. He dazzled the group with stories about medicine, with himself in the starring role. He dispensed free medical advice, making himself a hit with some of the group members.

Donna told him about a recent frightening experience with a child she was caring for in her home who had choked on a piece of toast.

"Well the kids started goofing around, you know, and Tommy had this big mouthful of toast. When he laughed, he sort of breathed in, and this whole wad of stuff got stuck in his throat. He started choking and trying to cough, but he couldn't. It was really stuck. I started pounding him on the back, like my mother had done when I was little, but it didn't do any good. In a few seconds, he started to turn blue, this sick, pale blue. It was hideous. But I guess you know all about that, Doctor.

"Well, anyway, here I am getting panicky. Tommy is sitting there in the chair turning blue, and I don't know what to do. I felt so helpless. I thought, this kid is going to die, and I don't know how to stop him. All the other kids were screaming and crying and looking at me.

"All of a sudden, this one rambunctious kid runs past me with his head lowered like a charging bull and rams his head into Tommy's middle, doubling him over, and out pops the toast. I was so helpless, and this little kid took over and saved Tommy. He told me he'd learned about it on a kid's TV show, but you're supposed to do it with your fists, he said, from behind the choking person. He said he didn't think he had time to do it right. I've had courses in first-aid, and that's the first thing they teach you. But at that moment I was just helpless, you know, and later I was ashamed."

Tears were rolling down Donna's cheeks. The group was trying to comfort her, but the young doctor just sat there in a kind of trance.

Noticing Gary's transfixed expression, the therapist asked, "Something you'd like to say, Gary?"

Startled out of his reverie, he said, "No, not really. Her story just reminded me of something. I'm not sure exactly, like I was that kid who saved the choking one. My mother was always kind of helpless when I was a kid, and I had to be the one to take charge."

"So even as a child, you were strong," the therapist mused. "Is it important to you to always be strong, Gary?"

"Well, yes. You have to be strong. Bad things happen if you're weak. Everybody knows that."

"Do bad things ever happen even when you're strong?" Donna asked.

Gary looked surprised, as if he didn't know how to answer. He thought a moment and said, "Well, I suppose so, but if you're strong, you can handle it."

"Have there been any times in your life when being strong hasn't handled it?" the therapist asked.

Thoughts of Jennie came rushing into Gary's head. He shifted in his chair, looked down at his hands, and crossed his legs.

"Gary, are there times in your life when being strong causes bad things to happen?" the therapist persisted.

"How can that be?" Gary responded, regaining his self-composure. "When you're strong, you can control things, have them your way."

"What about people? Can you always control other people?"

"If you're strong enough, I suppose you can," he sort of mumbled, as the group strained to hear his answer. Gary was embarrassed by all the attention, as if he had said something ridiculous.

The therapist had an idea. "Gary, would you be willing to try a little experiment with the group? It has to do with strength and weakness. I think we might all find it valuable."

"That depends," he answered hesitantly.

"It's really simple," the therapist explained. "You're a strong man physically. All you have to do is lie on the floor. Four of us will position ourselves on your arms and legs and try to hold you down. You try to get up. I want you to find out if strength can always control things, and if it can't what it feels like to really be helpless."

Gary smiled broadly. "Oh, is that all? I am pretty

strong physically, and I don't think just four of you can keep me down."

"That's fine," the therapist said. "Let's try it and see what happens. I want you to know, however, that this is just an exercise, and no one is trying to hurt you. If you want to stop, let us know, and we'll stop."

"Got it," Gary said with the same smile.

The group cleared a space on the floor as Gary removed his coat and tie. He lay on the carpet, arms and legs spread, and said, "Okay, folks, hop aboard for the ride of your life."

The four volunteers positioned themselves at each leg and arm. When everybody was ready, the therapist shouted, "All right, Gary, get up."

Instantly they felt a tremendous surge of power in Gary's muscles. But the group members exerted equal pressure downward and held him down. They were all straining, battling the man beneath them. He, too, was straining. His eyes were pinched shut, his jaw clenched tight. After a minute or so he relaxed. And so did the group. He took advantage of their relaxed grips and tried to raise himself up again, laughing nervously. But they responded with greater strength to keep him down. After a while, he had to relax once more. And so did the group.

Now he wasn't laughing. There was a change in his face. It showed, not fear, but grim determination, deadly seriousness. He wasn't playing anymore.

A third time he tensed and tried to buck them off. The group could feel a difference in this effort. It was strong, but almost desperately so. After a few seconds, his legs began to tremble, then they relaxed. Gary was breathing hard and fast. He was in trouble. He had overestimated his strength. His face changed again. Now it showed fear.

His last attempt also failed. Gary had lost.

Then he began to cry, at first quietly, then in huge deep sobs that seemed to come from a place way down inside him, perhaps a place he had not been to in a long time.

Arthur and Donna started to offer comfort, but the therapist motioned them away and quietly asked the group to step out of the room for a few minutes. When the therapist came back a few moments later, Gary was sitting in his chair, breathing heavily, but evenly.

"You okay?" the therapist asked.

"Yeah, yeah, I'm okay."

"Can you handle talking about it with the group?"

"I think so," he sighed.

After the group members were resettled in their places, the therapist asked Gary how he felt inside while he was struggling to get up.

"At first I couldn't believe it. I'm pretty strong. Lift weights, jog, work out. Then I got mad—really mad. Getting mad is usually enough. If I get seriously mad, then I can do what needs doing, and I do it. But this time, it didn't work. Then I got scared. One part of me knew you weren't going to hurt me, but another part was scared anyway. But what was really strange was that whenever I would relax, so would you. And the harder I tried to get you off of me and get up, the harder you worked against me."

"I think you may have discovered something that has intrigued me for years: the 'law of reversed effort,'" the therapist said. "Most of us usually think, as you do, Gary, that strength is the only way to achieve, to get things done. We strive and strive. But there are some things we cannot get by striving."

The therapist pulled two books from his shelf. Looking through one, he found what he wanted. "Alan Watts, in his book *The Wisdom of Insecurity*, talks about the law of reversed effort this way. Tell me if it matches your experience in our exercise?"

The therapist began to read: " 'When you try to stay on the surface of the water, you sink; but when you try to sink, you float' "[1] Is that how you felt, Gary?"

"Yes, that was exactly how it felt."

The therapist continued reading. "'When you hold your breath, you lose it—which immediately calls to mind an ancient and most neglected saying, "Whosoever would save his soul shall lose it." Insecurity is the result of trying to be secure, and, contrariwise, salvation and sanity consist in the most radical recognition that we have no way of saving ourselves.' And this passage is noteworthy, 'that to know the truth one must get rid of knowledge, and that nothing is more powerful and creative than emptiness—from which men shrink.'"[2]

"I was just thinking of my fiancée," Gary said. "I think she has been trying to tell me this for some time now, only I couldn't seem to hear it. I guess I've been working very hard to control her, to be strong for her, to direct everything. It almost broke us up. I've been hitting a lot of brick walls lately. I guess I need to back off and quit trying so hard."

"That's sort of what a character in Tolstoy's novel *Anna Karenina* discovered," the therapist announced enthusiastically. "Listen to this: 'He thought of nothing, wished for nothing . . . but to do his work as well as possible.' This character, Levin, is out working in the fields with the peasants. It's his land, and he wants very much to mow as well as they do. He doesn't want them to show him up."

The therapist read, "'' Levin lost all sense of time, and could not have told whether it was late or early now. A change began to come over his work, which gave him immense satisfaction. In the midst of his toil there were moments during which he forgot what he was doing, and it came all easy to him, and at those same moments his row was almost as smooth and well-cut as Tit's [one of the peasants]. But as soon as he recollected what he was doing, and began trying to do better, he was at once conscious of all the difficulty of his task, and the row was badly mown.'"[3]

Gary shed tears one more time in this group session. But at the same time there was a wonderful smile on his face.

"I think I've got it. I have a wonderful feeling inside, and I can't wait to see Jennie!"

NOTES

1. Alan Watts, *The Wisdom of Insecurity* (New York: Pantheon, 1951), pp. 9-10.
2. Ibid.
3. Leo Tolstoy, *Anna Karenina* (New York: Random House, 1966), p. 297

CHAPTER 16

Experiential Exercises to Overcome Manipulation*

Why do people manipulate? Many do so because they are beset by fear, fear of others and fear of expressing the truth of their feelings and desires. They are afraid that if others know the truth of their feelings and desires, they will be at the mercy of others. But manipulators are often selective about what they fear. Some who fear anger avoid conflict and confrontation with others. Others who fear love avoid closeness with others. And some fear being weak, while others fear being strong. It is the *denial of what we fear* that defines our manipulative style or pattern.

1. If you are *afraid of love*, you may be avoiding it with phony expressions of anger. You are predominantly aggressive in your dealings with others and play the role of the *blamer and attacker*. In doing so, you avoid closeness with others, but you also lose touch with your authentic anger.

---

*Adapted from Everett L. Shostrom and Tim Timmons, "Exercises for Overcoming Manipulation." Used by permission.

2. *If you are afraid of anger,* you may be avoiding it with phony expressions of love. You play the role of *pleaser and placater* in the belief that you can get what you want from others without confrontation and conflict. In doing so, you avoid feeling and expressing genuine anger, but you also lose touch with your authentic love.

3. If you are *afraid of being weak,* you may avoid any hint that you are "just a human being" with phony expressions of superiority. You play the role of *controller and dictator.* By refusing to allow others to be strong, you enhance only the appearance of your own strength. You thereby lose both the power of genuine strength and the opportunities for closeness with others that authentic vulnerability (weakness) brings.

4. If you are *afraid of being too strong,* you avoid responsibility with phony expressions of incompetence, weakness, and humility. You play the role of *avoider and withdrawer,* avoiding opportunities to display adequacy and withdrawing from participation with others. You fear that someone might expect more from you than you are willing to give. In doing so, you never have to perform (be strong). You are also seldom able to achieve, and you often overlook your genuine feelings of weakness.

Examples of manipulation:

Fear and Denial of   Lead to *Phony Expressions of*

Genuine Love....................Blaming & Attacking
Genuine Anger..................Pleasing & Placating
Genuine Weakness...... Controlling & Dictating
Genuine Strength......... Withrawing & Avoiding

Since manipulation is learned by experience in actual encounter with the world, it is important to overcome manipulation by similar methods. The methods cannot be simply intellectual, but must be experiential as well. Take the example of the young actor whose walk-on part required just one line. When a gun would fire, he was to say, "My God, I am shot!" No matter how much he applied himself in rehearsal, he just couldn't say his line with feeling and conviction. He wasn't *experiencing* the shock of a bullet hitting him. The director decided finally on a ruse. He would load the gun secretly with rock salt, hoping that when it hit, the wooden actor would "feel" his role. Came the night of the performance and the duffer's scene. He walked on, the gun fired, the rock salt stung. "My God!" he shrieked, "I really am shot!" But of course that wasn't the line.

To get immediate, honest response to your behavior, the following exercises have been devised for you to use with a partner. Do not be afraid to exaggerate your role playing. It will help to create a heightened experience and more awareness.

Each of these exercises deals with one of the polarities of your life experience: anger and love, strength and weakness. Each is designed to help you recognize the difference between manipulative, phony behavior and genuine expression. The first exercise in each section is designed to help you to experience your manipulative pattern, such as *blaming and attacking*. The second exercise in each section is to help you to experience the genuine expression of that polarity. The third exercise is to help you to experience the part of yourself you may have been avoiding in your relationships with others.

The Manipulators

I. Exercises for Blamers and Attackers
   A. Start out by experiencing your *blaming and attacking* behavior. *Tell your partner:* "You never do anything right! It's all your fault!"
   B. Experience *genuine anger* (assertion) that is communicative and non-destructive.
   Tell your partner: "I'm very upset about this situation and want us both to work on improving it."
   C. Experience *genuine caring* that you may have been avoiding with your blaming and attacking behavior. As children, most people were touched by their parents; at moments of greatest tenderness a mother or father would touch the child on the face.
   Tell your partner: "I really care for you." (With your fingertips gently stroke your partner's hair, forehead, closed eyes, nose, cheeks, lips, and chin as you softly name each feature. Ask your partner to respond to you with the same words and touch.)

II. Exercises for Pleasers and Placaters
   A. Start by experiencing your *pleasing and placating* behavior.
   Tell your partner: "It's no problem. No matter how much work it is for me, I know how much it means to you."
   B. Experience your *genuine caring* as appreciation for another instead of placating another.
   Tell your partner: "I want to do this for you. It feels good to help."

C. Experience the *genuine anger* (assertion) you may have been avoiding with your pleasing and placating manipulations.
Tell your partner: "No! I won't!"
Your partner responds: "Yes! Yes, you will!"
(Repeat back and forth several times until you feel convinced you can say no.)

III. Exercises for Controllers and Dictators
A. Start by experiencing your *controlling and dictating behavior*. *Tell your partner*: "Quit being so upset. Take it easy! You should be calm!"
B. Experience your *genuine strength* instead of control.
Tell your partner: "I *feel* as if you are upset. Can I help out?"
C. Experience your *genuine vulnerability* that you may have been avoiding.
Work with your partner: Stand with your back against a smooth wall with your feet planted approximately fifteen inches from the wall. Ask your partner to stand in front of you, ready to help you the second you ask. Gradually bend your knees and slowly lower your back down the wall. You will feel discomfort and weakness in your legs. Stand it as long as you can. Then reach out to your partner for support and help. Your partner should hold your hands and support your body as you slide down to the floor. Notice that the pain and weakness, with your partner's help, begin to go away.

The Manipulators

IV. Exercise for Withdrawers and Avoiders
 A. Start by experiencing your *withdrawing and avoiding* behavior.
   Tell your partner: "I can't do it. I don't know how. Just leave me alone."
 B. Experience your *genuine weakness* (vulnerability) instead of your manipulative avoidance of responsibility.
   Tell your partner: "I want to be able to do this, but I need your help and support to get me started."
 C. Experience your *genuine strength* (self-empowerment), which you may have been avoiding.
   Tell your partner: "I am able to stand on my own two feet!" (Keep repeating as you stamp your feet on the floor.)

Experiencing the realness in yourself—in your loving and in your anger, in your weakness and in your strength—is truly a gift you can give yourself that is beyond all measure.

Notice: Psychological tests of both actualization and manipulation for use by qualifying professionals in education, psychiatry, psychology, and counseling are available from EDITS/Educational and Industrial Testing Service, P.O. Box 7234, San Diego, CA 92107, phone (619) 488-1666. The tests of actualization are the *Personal Orientation Inventory* (POI), 1963, by Everett L. Shostrom, Ph.D. and the *Personal Orientation Dimensions* (POD), 1975, by Everett L. Shostrom, Ph.D. The test of manipulation is the *Manipulation Orientation Dimensions* (MOD), 1990, by Everett L. Shostrom, Ph.D. and Tim Timmons.

Index

Index